Intellectual Property Law

Cavendish
Publishing
Limited

First published in Great Britain 1999 by Cavendish Publishing Limited, The Glass House, Wharton Street, London WC1X 9PX, United Kingdom

Telephone: +44 (0) 171 278 8000 Facsimile: +44 (0) 171 278 8080

e-mail: info@cavendishpublishing.com

Visit our Home Page on http://www.cavendishpublishing.com

British Library Cataloguing in Publication Data

Intellectual property law – (Lawcard)

1 Intellectual property – Great Britain

346.4'1'048

ISBN 1 85941 435 4

Printed and bound in Great Britain

Contents

4 Copyright 54

1 Remedies

Intellectual property rights can only be enforced through the courts.

A range of orders and remedies are available, the most important of which are:

(a) injunctions, which need to be considered in almost every case;

(b) damages.

Injunctions

Injunctions are orders from the courts prohibiting a party from pursuing a wrongful course of conduct.

Injunctions are equitable and given at the discretion of the court.

The injunction is the most frequently used pre-trial order and is the preferred remedy in most cases as it prevents an infringer from exploiting the intellectual property of another.

Like most civil cases, an intellectual property dispute may not go as far as trial, and a case will often be settled by negotiation or a licensing agreement.

The leading case is *American Cyanamid v Ethicon* (1975) (which involved a patent for a dissolving medical stitch).

It was held that, in determining whether to grant an interlocutory injunction or not (ie, the exercise of the court's discretion), the following factors must be addressed:

(a) Is there a serious issue to be tried?

(b) Can the plaintiff show a strong *prima facie* case?

(c) Would damages be a suitable remedy for the plaintiff?

(d) Could the plaintiff adequately compensate the defendant with damages?

(e) If the above factors are equal, the courts must decide, on the balance of convenience, which party is likely to suffer most.

Figure 1.1

Injunctions – relevant factors

✔ **Discretionary**

✔ **Serious issue**

✔ **Damages not a remedy**

✔ **Balance of convenience**

✔ **Status quo**

Generally, the courts will act to preserve the status quo and grant the injunction in favour of the plaintiff.

Damages will not be a suitable remedy where the wrong is:

(a) irreparable;

(b) outside the scope of financial compensation;

(c) very difficult to calculate (eg, damage to reputation).

Figure 1.2

INTERLOCUTORY INJUNCTION

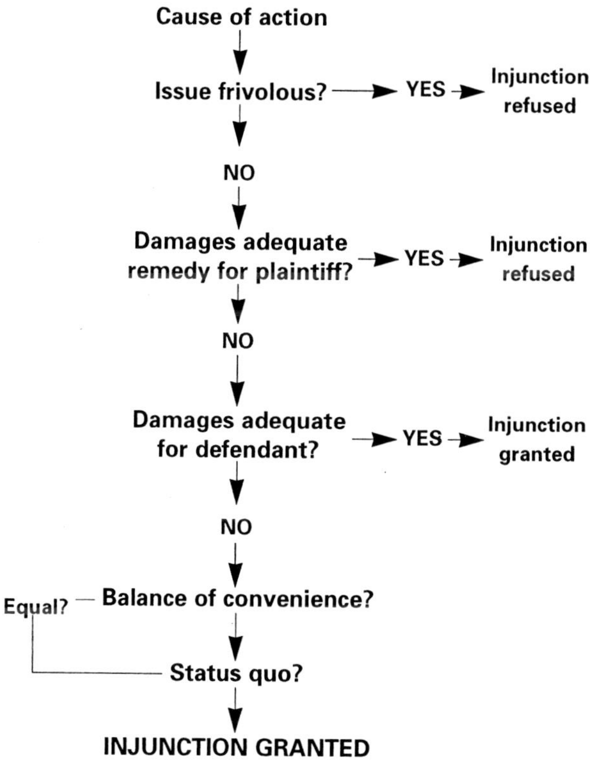

Cause of action

↓

Issue frivolous? → YES → Injunction refused

↓

NO

↓

Damages adequate remedy for plaintiff? → YES → Injunction refused

↓

NO

↓

Damages adequate for defendant? → YES → Injunction granted

↓

NO

↓

Equal? — **Balance of convenience?**

↓

Status quo?

↓

INJUNCTION GRANTED

In *American Cyanamid*, it was considered less harmful to restrain a new activity than to undermine an established one. In *Cayne v Global Natural Resources plc* (1984), the balance of convenience was taken to mean the balance of the risk of doing injustice.

The penalties for a breach of an injunction include committal to prison or a fine.

Inability to pay damages due to financial weakness may be a reason to grant an injunction (*Missing Link Software v Magee* (1989)).

In *Series 5 Software v Philip Clarke and Others* (1995), reviewing these principles, the court stated the discretionary nature of injunctive relief. It was emphasised that the court should not try to resolve difficult matters of fact and law at an early stage.

Injunctions may be granted against a non-infringer in intellectual property cases.

In *Norwich Pharmaceutical Co v Commrs of Customs and Excise* (1974), following earlier authority, it was held that:

> ... if a man has in his possession or control goods, the dissemination of which ... will infringe another's patent or trade mark, he becomes, as soon as he is aware of this fact, subject to a duty (an equitable duty) not to allow those goods to pass out of his possession.

The courts may refuse an injunction where a transaction is an isolated one and there is no likelihood of repetition (*Leahy, Kelly and Leahy v Glover* (1893)).

Further principles that a court may apply are set out in *Shelfer v City of London Electric Lighting Co* (1895). Relief may be denied:

(a) if the injury to the plaintiff's legal rights is small; and

(b) it is one which is capable of being estimated in money; and

(c) it is one which can be adequately compensated by a small money payment; and

(d) it would be oppressive to the defendant to grant an injunction.

Then damages in substitution for an injunction may be given. The purpose of an injunction may also be considered – not to stop a continued flow of a wrongful benefit arising from the breach, but to prevent a continuation of the breach of confidence.

The courts may also look to *Armstrong v Sheppard & Short Ltd* (1959), where Lord Evershed MR confirmed an injunction might not lie where a wrong is trivial.

Pre-trial orders
An Anton Piller order allows the seizure of infringing goods or documents where there is a danger that a defendant may hide or destroy the evidence.

In *Anton Piller KG v Manufacturing Processes* (1975), Ormrod J held that a plaintiff must be able to show:

(a) a strong *prima facie* case;

(b) the damage, whether actual or potential, must be very serious for the plaintiff;

(c) there must be clear evidence that the defendants have, in their possession, documents or objects and that there is a real possibility they may destroy such materials.

In *Columbia Picture Industries v Robinson* (1986), it was held that the plaintiff must show a strong case for infringement of his rights and that potential damage is serious.

Figure 1.3

If plaintiff can show:

strong case

+

serious harm

+

**defendant has
infringing items**

+

**likelihood of evidence   ANTON
being destroyed   ────────▶   PILLER
                                        ORDER**

Damages

Damages are often sought by plaintiffs in intellectual property cases, in addition to injunctions.

Damages are generally available for all breaches of intellectual property rights, though they may be limited by statute and case law. The measure of damages is normally tortious, ie, the aim is to put the injured party back in the position he would have enjoyed had the injury never taken place.

Factors that may be considered in assessing damages are:

(a) whether the plaintiff would have charged a licence fee for the work; and

(b) would he have expected a royalty.

Account of profits

As an alternative to damages, the plaintiff may claim an account of profits, an equitable remedy whereby the plaintiff claims the profit that the defendant has made on each infringing item.

An account of profits recovers the unjust enrichment that the plaintiff has obtained. It is a technical and expensive remedy, involving professional scrutiny of accounts. Difficulties may arise with establishing the date from which the assessment may run (see *Potton v Yorkshire* (1990)).

Delivery up

Where a plaintiff obtains a final injunction, the courts may include an order for delivery up of the infringing articles.

See ss 99, 114 of the Copyright, Designs and Patents Act 1988 (CDPA); s 61 of the Patents Act 1977 (PA).

The order may also encompass the destruction of the goods or the obliteration of an offending mark from goods.

Criminal sanctions

In addition, to civil remedies, the law provides criminal sanctions for various infringing acts.

A plaintiff is entitled to take civil action and commence criminal proceedings simultaneously (*Thames Hudson Ltd v Design and Artists Copyright Society Ltd* (1995); *R v Bridgeman and Butt* (1995)).

Criminal sanctions exist as follows:

- copyright: ss 107–10 and s 207 (fraudulent reception) of the CDPA 1988;

- trade marks: s 92 of the Trade Marks Act 1994;

- patents: ss 110–11 of the PA 1977.

2 Confidential information

The action for breach of confidence – basic elements

The basis for an action for breach of confidence may lie in equity or contract or at common law.

No right to privacy under English common law exists, although Art 8 of the European Convention on Human Rights seeks to guarantee a limited right with respect to the private life of individuals and families and to protect correspondence.

Figure 2.1

Categories of protectable information

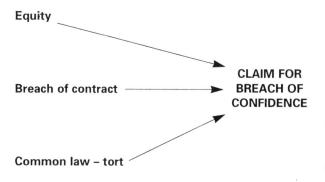

To be protected, information must have 'the necessary quality of confidence about it, namely it must not be something which is public property and public knowledge'

(*per* Lord Greene MR in *Saltman Engineering Co Ltd v Campbell Engineering Co Ltd* (1963)).

Examples

Personal secrets:	*Argyll v Argyll* (1967)
Commercial records:	*Anton Piller KG v Manufacturing Processes Ltd* (1976)
Trade secrets:	*Seager v Copydex* (1967)
Government secrets:	*AG v Guardian Newspapers* (1990)

In *Coco Engineers v Clark* (1969), Megarry VC expressed the view that the doctrine of confidential information would only be used in cases of sufficient gravity and not mere 'tittle-tattle'. Matters that are revealed to the public, such as by a court case, cease to be public (*Chantry Martin v Martin* (1953)).

A person receiving confidential information is still under an obligation of confidence, even if he already knows the information (*Johnson v Heat and Air Systems Ltd* (1941)).

However, confidentiality may still be maintained even though the information has been published, to prevent further damage through repetition (see *Schering Chemicals v Falman Ltd* (1982)).

Liability may sometimes attach to recipients who innocently acquire confidential information; liability arises at the time a party is informed of the breach of confidence (see *Stephenson Jordan v MacDonald & Evan* (1951); *Printers & Finishers v Holloway (No 2)* (1965)).

The broadly worded formulations for the elements of breach of confidence, adopted by the courts in the past, have tended to encourage plaintiffs. In *Coco Engineers v Clark* (1969), Megarry VC held the following to be necessary for an action:

(a) information must have a necessary element of confidentiality – it is of a type to be protected;

(b) the information was communicated in circumstances of an obligation of confidentiality; and

(c) there is a risk of the information being used in an unauthorised way, possibly causing damage.

Figure 2.2

Coco v Clark (1969)

- **Important information**

- **Obligation of confidence**

- **Risk of damage**

The *Coco* case is frequently cited and partly followed the approach of the Court of Appeal in *Saltman Engineering Co Ltd v Campbell Engineering Co Ltd* (1948). There is no need for an obligation of confidence to be in writing, as the courts have been prepared to imply terms.

Prototypes and ideas

Designs, prototypes or product samples shown to others prior to any business deal may be protected, but subject to the decision in *Carflow Products (UK) Ltd v Linwoood Securities (Birmingham) Ltd and Others* (1996), where the court refused to impose an obligation of confidence on the party viewing the sample.

It was held that there are two possible approaches to the question of whether a disclosure was in confidence:

(a) subjective, ie, what did the parties themselves think they were doing by way of imposing or accepting obligations? And

(b) objective, ie, what would a reasonable man think they were doing?

As equity looked at the conscience of the individual, the subjective view was the appropriate one.

Merely because a prototype was being offered for sale, did not import an obligation of confidence.

In a passage from the *Coco* case, Megarry J suggested that an objective test could apply in situations where:

> ... information of commercial or industrial value is given on a businesslike basis and with some avowed common object in mind, such as a joint venture or the manufacture of articles by one party for the other.

He stated that he would regard the recipient of the information 'as carrying a heavy burden if he seeks to repel a contention that he was bound by an obligation of confidence'.

It is presumed that the reasonable man will know about other intellectual property rights when viewing a prototype, but he need not assume he is placing himself under an obligation of confidence in respect of the matter that could be protected independently.

Ideas may be protected by confidential information (*Gilbert v Star Newspaper Co Ltd* (1894)).

A claim in confidential information may assist in situations where copyright is of no assistance (*Frazer v Thames Television* (1984) – idea for the 'Rock Follies' series).

However, in *De Maudsley v Palumbo and Others* (1996), the courts refused the claim of the plaintiff for breach of confidence involving his idea for a night club. It was held that to attain the status of confidential information an idea must:

(a) contain some significant element of originality;

(b) be clearly identifiable (as an idea of the confider);

(c) be of potential commercial attractiveness;

(d) be sufficiently well developed to be capable of actual realisation.

In *Maudsley v Palumbo*, the idea had first been raised at a supper party where the plaintiff communicated his ideas for a night club which he claimed had a number of novel features. The plaintiff claimed that the defendants were subsequently in breach by opening a 'Ministry of Sound' club along such lines without his permission.

Figure 2.3

Personal secrets

However, while the courts may be taking a more restrictive approach to confidential information in employment or business contexts, different considerations may apply in cases involving personal privacy. In *Barrymore v News Group Newspapers Ltd* (1997) (a case which involved the actor Michael Barrymore seeking to restrain release of information about his personal life, from a former sexual partner, to tabloid newspapers), it was held that common sense dictated that, when people entered into a personal relationship of this nature, it was not done for the purpose of publication in newspapers; the information about the relationship was for those involved in such a relationship and not for some wider purposes.

Nevertheless, if a plaintiff has courted publicity, a claim may be rejected (see *Lennon v News Group Newspapers Ltd* (1978); *Khashoggi v Smith* (1980)).

Employment

Confidentiality cases often arise in the context of terms of employment.

In *Faccenda Chicken v Fowler* (1985), at issue was the right to restrain information obtained during the operation of a contract of employment. The Court of Appeal held that information could be divided into three categories:

(a) information of a general or trivial type which was not confidential;

(b) information that was the employee's 'stock in trade' – working knowledge which remains confidential while the contract of employment remains in force; this obligation ceases once employment ends and any restriction should be based on an anti-competition clause;

(c) information that was so sensitive (eg, formulae, trade secrets) that it could never lose its designation and a duty of confidence existed whether employment had ceased or not.

Figure 2.4

Faccenda Chicken v Fowler (1985)

(a) Trivial =   **not protectable**

(b) 'Stock in trade' =   **protectable during employment**

(c) Trade secrets =   **always protected**

As was identified in *Printers & Finishers Ltd v Holloway* (1965), the key test as to whether information learned by an employee is capable of protection is whether:

> ... the information in question can fairly be regarded as a separate part of the employee's stock of knowledge which a man of ordinary intelligence and honesty would recognise to be the property of his employer, and not his own to do as he likes with.

However, *Ocular Sciences Ltd and Another v Aspect Vision Care Ltd & Others* (1997) shows that:

(a) bare assertions by employers that matters are secret or confidential will not be sufficient where an employer seeks to restrain the use of information taken away by a departing employee; and

(b) even where a claim of confidential information may succeed, the court can still refuse an injunction – effectively defeating the main purpose of bringing the claim in the first place.

In *Ocular Sciences Ltd*, the two plaintiffs sued eight defendants for breach of confidence, procuring such a breach, breach of contract, breach of fiduciary duty, conspiracy and infringement of copyright and design rights relating to the manufacture of contact lenses.

Laddie J questioned the validity of the categorisation of information type (a) in *Faccenda Chicken*, stating 'what an employee can or cannot make available to a competitor during the period of his employment has little to do with the law of confidence', again implying that employment law principles, such as duties of good faith, are more relevant. (This raises the possibility of claims against employees for releasing information hitherto classed as general or trivial.)

Laddie J considered that an ex-employee is entitled to use and put at the disposal of a new employer all acquired skill and knowledge, regardless of where he acquired it. Indeed, he recognised a public interest in an employee being able to do so in cases of dispute, and that public interests should prevail over those of the former employer.

It follows that, to succeed in an action for breach of confidence once employment ceases, the employer will have to prove that the secret is one which should never be released, whatever the circumstances, 'information which, in the *Coco v Clark* sense [(c)], is confidential'.

As was recognised by the Court of Appeal in *Lancashire Fires v SA Lyons & Co Ltd and Others* (1996), the boundaries between categories of information may be hard to detect (cited in *Ocular Services*).

It was held that the normal presumption was that information which employees obtained without having to memorise specific documents could be taken away by them and used to the benefit of future employers.

A bare assertion by an employer during employment that a matter is secret is not enough.

The subjective view of an employer of what constitutes a trade secret is not decisive. There has to be something that is objectively a trade secret, but which is known or ought to be known by both parties.

As was recognised in *Lancashire Fires*, in the absence of a clear dividing line, except where 'secrecy' of the process or component was obvious from its very nature, the onus was on employers to define expressly those parts of their operations that they regarded as entitled to protection. If this was not practicable, the appropriate response was a contractual restraint on competitive activity after end of employment.

The decision in *Ocular Sciences* gives rise to the following propositions :

(a) broad statements in earlier judgments may not automatically be relied upon;

(b) the obligation of confidence must be precisely identified;

(c) the alleged confidential information itself needs to be capable of precise identification and be distinguishable from non-confidential information;

(d) where the interests of the public and the employer collide, the former prevails;

(e) a plaintiff needs to be aware that an injunction may not be forthcoming.

Public interest

The question of public interest in *Ocular Sciences* is one which has developed as an important defence in breach of confidence actions.

Since the 1960s, the courts have increasingly indicated that a claim of public interest may justify the breach of the obligation of confidence.

Several of the cases overlap with copyright infringement.

To allow the publication of confidential information, a defendant must do more than raise a bare plea of public interest – it is necessary to show a legitimate ground that it is in the public interest for the matter to be disclosed.

Both equity and the common law recognised the obligation of good faith to an employer. In *Gartside v Outram* (1856), it was stated that:

> The true doctrine is that there is no confidence as to the disclosure of an iniquity. No private obligations can dispense with that universal one that lies on every member of society to discover every design which may be formed, contrary to the laws of society, to destroy the public welfare.

Typically, it was used in cases involving the exposure of unlawful acts of an employer.

In the 20th century, the modern law of a public interest defence is taken as commencing with the authority of *Initial Services v Putterill* (1967), where price fixing agreements contrary to law were exposed. The Court of Appeal refused to strike out a defence of public interest. Lord Denning took the view that a defence of public interest was not limited to crime or fraud, but extended to any misconduct of such a nature that it ought, in the public interest, to be disclosed to others. Lord Salmon considered that what was an iniquity in 1856 might be too wide or too narrow a test to apply in 1967.

In *Frazer v Evans* (1968), Lord Denning considered that 'iniquity' was not the fundamental issue underlying the public interest, but was only an example of a new test, stating that there were some things which may be required to be disclosed in the public interest and to which no confidentiality doctrine could be applied.

The defence of public interest was raised in *Hubbard v Vosper* (1972), where the public interest was exposing the harm of quack remedies promoted by the Scientology movement, revealed by a former member of the organisation.

In *Beloff v Pressdram* (1973), the court recognised that the defence of public interest was established in law, but declined to apply it in a case involving leaked documents from *The Observer* newspaper to the satirical magazine *Private Eye*. 'Public interest' was taken to mean threats to national security, breach of law, fraud and matters medically dangerous and 'doubtless other misdeeds of similar gravity'.

The reluctance to extend the doctrine was based on the corresponding recognition by the courts that there is a public interest in keeping matters secret.

The courts have had to balance these requirements in a number of cases, including the following:

- *British Steel Corp v Granada TV* (1981): the media and the journalists who wrote for it had no immunity based on public interest protecting them from the obligation to disclose their sources of information in a court of law;

- *Malone Metropolitan Police Commrs* (1979): the plaintiff claimed that telephone tapping could result in the breach of confidential information. Breach of confidentiality in cases of telephone interception were held to be acceptable if necessary in the detection of crime;

- *Cork v McVicar* (1984): related to potential corruption by police; it was held that this was a situation where the passing of information to the press could be justified;

- *Francome v Mirror Group Newspapers* (1984): concerned an allegation that breach of jockey club rules should have been disclosed to the police or the jockey club. *The Daily Mirror* was not an acceptable destination for the information;

- *Lion Laboratories Ltd v Evans* (1985): concerned the results of a laboratory test in a confidential report indicating defects in a new breathalyser.

The *Lion* case was the first case to succeed that did not involve an iniquity. The Court of Appeal recognised that there was a public interest in a serious issue affecting the life of citizens and the risk of wrongful convictions based upon potentially unreliable recordings of the breathalyser. The public interest in this becoming known justified the breach of confidence.

Stephenson LJ set out the following criteria that were relevant to a court when determining an issue:

(a) the public may be interested in matters which are not their concern;

(b) the media has its own interest (as stated in *Francome v Mirror Group Newspapers* (1984)) and they are particularly vulnerable to the error of confusing the public interest with their own interest;

(c) the best recipient for information may not be the police or other responsible body.

In *Lion Laboratories v Evans* (1985), there was no evidence of 'iniquity' on the facts of the case, but a wider public interest could be identified in the proper administration of justice. *Malone* and *Francome* both involved allegations of an iniquity. As part of the process, the Court of Appeal confirmed that there is a strong public interest in preserving confidentiality within any business to allow it to be able to rely on its employees. The approach of the Court of Appeal is to ask whether a serious defence of public interest may succeed at trial.

Stephenson LJ held that the courts should not countenance disloyalty or breach of trust. Griffiths LJ held that the defence is not a mole's charter, and that there is often a strong case for maintaining the status quo.

In *Ocular Sciences*, a further extension of public interest was made in the employment context, in that an ex-employee was held entitled to use and put at the disposal of a new employer all acquired skill and knowledge, regardless of where he acquired it.

Figure 2.5

Lion Laboratories v Evans (1985)

(a)   **Public interest in issue**

(b)   **Media interest**

(c)   **Alternative recipients**

=   **factors to be weighed in determining public interest and defence**

Damages

The action for breach of confidence must be brought for damages on a tortious basis (*Seager v Copydex Ltd (No 2)* (1967)).

In *Dowson v Mason Potter* (1986), the Court of Appeal considered that damages should be based on the market value arising from a presumed willing seller and willing buyer.

In cases where a plaintiff would not have parted with the information, but instead would have retained it (eg, manufacturing formulae), loss of profits would be preferable.

When considering interlocutory injunctive relief, the court may apply the same approach as in defamation cases and decline the grant of an injunction if the defendant intends to justify (see *Woodward v Hutchins* (1977)). However, each case will turn on its facts and, in an action, the court will weigh the competing claims of confidence against those in favour of disclosure.

An injunction will only be granted if the confidential information can be identified with some precision (*Lock International plc v Beswick* (1987).

Injunctions in confidentiality

Even though some claims for breach of confidence may be upheld at a trial, the courts may, nonetheless, refuse to grant an injunction as it is not awarded as of right (see *Ocular Sciences* (injunction denied)).

Shelfer v City of London Electric Lighting Co (1895) decided that relief may be denied:

(a) if the injury to the plaintiff's legal rights is small; and

(b) it is one which is capable of being estimated in money; and

(c) it is one which can be adequately compensated by a small money payment; and

(d) it would be oppressive to the defendant to grant an injunction,

then damages in substitution for an injunction may be given. The court also considered the purpose of an injunction – not to stop continued flow of a wrongful benefit arising from the breach, but to prevent a continuation of the breach of confidence.

Figure 2.6

Damages – tortious basis

= market value of information

3 Patents

A patent is a monopoly right in an invention.

Patent law is regulated by the Patents Act 1977 (PA), although decisions under the Patent Act 1949 continue to aid interpretation. The UK is also a signatory to the European Patent Convention, incorporated into the PA 1977, which is also applicable.

A grant of a patent gives a monopoly in an invention for 20 years (s 25 of the PA 1977).

Applications for patents are made to the Patents Office, under the control of the comptroller, with rights of appeal to the Patent Tribunal and the courts. The comptroller may determine questions of applications and foreign and convention patents (ss 8–12 of the PA 1977).

Section 1 of the PA 1977 sets out the requirements of a patentable invention.

An invention must meet four criteria:

(a) it must be new (novelty);

(b) there must be an inventive step;

(c) it must be capable of industrial application;

(d) it must be an invention – not involving excluded material (s 1(1) of the PA 1977).

If the patent does not satisfy these conditions, no patent will be granted. If a party in a court case can prove that a patent

existing lacks any one (or more) of these criteria, the patent
will be invalid.

Figure 3.1

SECTION 1 OF THE PATENTS ACT 1977

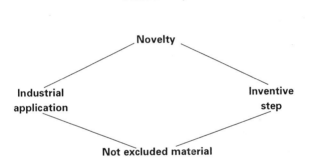

There are two types of patentable invention:

(a) product inventions; and

(b) process inventions.

Issues of patentability may arise either in connection with
the grant of a patent or in a counterclaim in infringement
proceeedings.

Exclusions from patentability

A number of matters are excluded from patentability on
grounds of unsuitability, the existence of other methods of

intellectual property law protection, public policy and morality. These exclusions cover:

(a) discoveries, scientific theories, mathematical models;

(b) literary, dramatic, musical or artistic works;

(c) schemes, rules, games, computer programs;

(d) the presentation of information;

(e) methods of medical treatment;

(f) those which, by publication or exploitation, might result in offensive, immoral or anti-social behaviour;

(g) plants and animals or any essential biological process not being a microbiological process.

Figure 3.2

ALTERNATIVE INTELLECTUAL PROPERTY PROTECTION – EXCLUDED MATERIAL

Discoveries and theories	**Confidential information**
Literary and artistic works	**Copyright**
Computer programs	**Copyright**
Schemes and games and information	**Copyright in expression**
Medical treatment	**N/A**
Public policy	**N/A**
Plants and animals plant varieties	**N/A although some protected**

Examples

Young v Rosenthal & Co (1884) 'an invention of an idea or mathematical formulae or anything of that sort could not be the subject of a patent'.

Medical methods and techniques of treatment of disease are not patentable, but new products such as drugs may be patentable (*Wyeth & Brother Ltd's Application and Schering AG's Application* (1985)). While the composition drug may be the subject of a patent, the instructions for taking a drug will not be patentable.

A substance that has previously been patented can be patented a second time for a medical use (*Wyeth & Brother Ltd's Application and Schering AG's Application*).

A method of flying an aeroplane was not patentable in *Rolls Royce Ltd's Application* (1963).

A system for arranging navigational buoys was not patentable (*W's Application* (1914)).

New rules for the card game 'Canasta' were not patentable (*Cobianchi's Application* (1953)).

The Secretary of State for Trade and Industry may vary what may be patented (s 1(5) of the PA 1977).

Computer programs

Computer programs 'as such' are excluded from patentability unless the program makes a contribution to the art which is technical in that a new invention arises with the computer as programmed.

In *Vicom Systems Inc's Application* (1987) to the European Patent Office (EPO), it was held that what was decisive with a computer program was what technical contribution the invention makes to the known art.

This approach has been followed in *Wang Laboratories Inc's Application* (1991), the court rejecting the claim on the basis that an existing machine with a new program did not combine to create a new computer (see *Fujitsu* (1996)).

Figure 3.3

PATENT PROTECTION – COMPUTER PROGRAMS

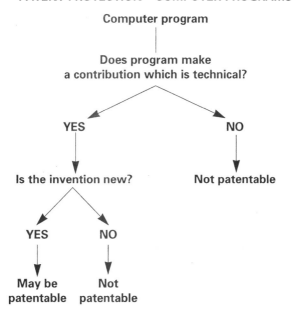

INTELLECTUAL PROPERTY LAW

Novelty

Section 2 requires an invention to be new.

To determine whether an invention is new, one considers the 'state of the art' at the priority date of the invention (ie, the date on which the patent was applied for (s 2(1) of the PA 1977).

The 'state of the art' is taken to include all information and material made available to the public in the UK or the rest of the world, whether in writing, orally, by use, or in any other way which is available to the public. If invention does not form part of the state of the art, it will be new.

If a patent can be said to be anticipated – someone else has thought of it and publicised it – the invention will be deprived of novelty.

A key question is disclosure – has the invention been made known to the public?

If so, the patent will probably fail for lack of novelty. But if a product or process has been kept secret, another inventor may be able to obtain a patent if he has independently reached the same result, providing all the other elements of patentability are present.

Once an invention has entered into the public domain, it cannot be patented: this is a rule of long standing (*Patterson v Gas Light and Coke and Co* (1877)).

Under s 3 of the PA 1977, the invention must actually be disclosed.

The receipt of a single specification by a patent agent in the UK was held to be a sufficient publication (*Bristol Myers Co's Application* (1969)).

Figure 3.4

NOVELTY

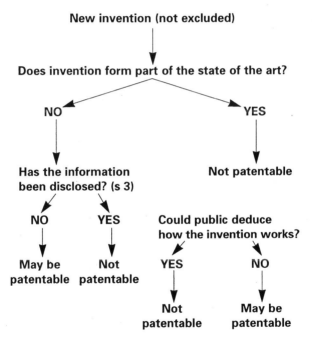

Disclosure may arise through prior publication of the invention (eg, in a relevant journal).

Japan Styrene Paper/Foam Particles (1991) makes it irrelevant that no one ever read it or knew about it.

Suggestions that a skilled person would not read some material are also rejected -- the assumption is that the notional skilled man is sufficiently interested to bother.

The document must actually disclose the invention to a competent person and reveal principles which underlie the invention to such an extent that a competent reader could take steps to reproduce the invention.

If the invention as already described or published would amount to an infringement if put into use after the patent has been granted, the patentee's invention cannot be novel.

A test of novelty proposed in *General Tyre v Firestone* (1972) is that, if a document contains a clear description of the invention or the instructions to do or make something that would infringe the patent if carried out after the grant of the patent, it would amount to an infringement.

It must be something which falls within the claims of the patent and not simply something that might be an infringement:

> A signpost, however clear, upon the road to the patentee's invention will not suffice. The prior inventor must be clearly shown to have planted his flag as the precise destination before the patentee.

A statement that an invention will not work will not destroy novelty, nor will it if the disclosure is capable of more than one interpretation. An invention can be anticipated by a single drawing, but generally more will be needed. Special rules exist for photographs (*Van der Lely (C) NV v Bamford Ltd* (1963)).

The possibility that members of the public may have seen the invention on display may be a factor which undermines novelty (*Prout v British Gas* (1992); *Lux Traffic Controls Ltd v Pike Signals Ltd* (1993)).

Similarly, where the invention is used in public, it will fail for lack of novelty if the public may deduce how the invention works.

Circuitry of a computer is not disclosed if it is inside the computer and cannot be seen by members of the public (*Quantel v Spaceward* (1990)).

Novelty will not arise simply where an inventor puts together a collection of old integers in a new or unusual way (*Pugh v Riley Cycle Co* (1914)). A new use for an old idea does not confer novelty (*Molins v Industrial Machinery Co Ltd* (1938)).

Disclosures do not undermine novelty for a six month period where either:

- the information was obtained unlawfully or in breach of confidence (eg, industrial espionage);

- the disclosure resulted from display by the inventor at a prescribed international exhibition and the applicant files proper notification of this (only exhibitions to educate the public occurring every 20 years fall within this);

- substances and compositions involved in treatment which do not form part of the state of the art.

See s 2(4).

Inventive step

Under s 3 of the PA 1977, an invention involves an inventive step if it is not obvious to a person skilled in the art.

This test requires presuming a notionally skilled individual and what he would have predicted or anticipated as the next obvious stage in the development of the technology concerned. The notionally skilled person is not presumed to be imaginative or inventive himself. All factual information is relevant.

The notional skilled person is assumed to read all the relevant material. Basically, the court is asking: was the invention obvious – without any inventive element or effort – or did it require more?

With novelty, the court is enquiring whether the invention is actually known. With inventive steps, the court has to determine whether the invention was obvious or predictable – the next step in development from the state of the art. The courts will not prevent a person from doing what is an obvious extension of existing technical knowledge, if sufficiently interested (*PLG v Ardon International* (1995)).

The level of invention need only be very low. A mere scintilla of invention will be sufficient (*Parkes v Crocker* (1929)). Providing it can be detected, an inventive step will held to be present.

Discovery by accident does not deprive an invention of patentability (*Crane v Price* (1842)). Nor is it relevant whether the inventor recognises at the time that an invention has been made (*British United Shoe Manufacturer v Fussell* (1908)). Where skilled individuals have failed to come up with an answer, it will be difficult to suggest an invention is obvious (see *Parks-Cramer v Thornton* (1966)).

The question of whether an inventive step is present is determined with reference to a notional worker skilled, but unimaginative, in the art. Sometimes, the notionally skilled worker is taken to be the equivalent of several workers or a research team, or deemed to possess skills of several disciplines (*Boehringer Mannheim v Genzyme* (1993)).

The notionally skilled worker is taken to have the common general knowledge of the art at the date of the invention and to be familiar with the relevant literature in the field when considering an answer to a particular problem.

The courts are wary of hindsight. In *Technograph Printed Circuits Ltd v Mills and Rockley (Electronics) Ltd* (1972), it was recognised that it is:

> ... only because the invention has been made and has proved successful that it is possible to postulate what starting point and by what particular combination of steps the inventor could have reached his invention.

In proceedings, the court or tribunal usually relies on the evidence of expert witnesses to determine inventive step.

Tests for the inventive step

If the old art clearly anticipates the new, there will be no inventive step.

Various tests have been applied over the years and there are trends and fashions in judicial approach.

In *General Tyre and Rubber Co v Firestone* (1972), Graham J reviewed previous authorities on obviousness, holding it relevant ask following questions:

(a) Does the invention have technical or commercial value?

(b) Does the invention involve a new use for an old thing? If the invention is a simple extension of a known thing there will be no inventive step (*Reikmann v Thierry* (1897); *Isola v Thermos* (1910)).

(c) Does the invention satisfy a long-felt want (*Longbottom v Shaw* (1891))? A history of failed attempts to reach a desired goal will be evidence of an inventive step, even if the invention is simple (*Parks Cramer v Thornton* (1966)).

(d) Is the invention commercial successfully? (NB: this may not be determinative – clever advertising or marketing might be responsible).

(e) Have independent researchers reached the same result (*Johns Electric Ind Mfy Ltd v Mabuch 1 Motor KK* (1996)?

(f) Identification of the problem and formulating its solution from known features may amount to inventiveness (the 'workmate' in *Hickman v Andrews* (1983)).

(g) Selection of the research area. In *Re Beecham Group's Ltd (Amoxycillin) Application* (1980) it was held that the selection of a particular line or direction of enquiry can be evidence of inventive skill.

Merely because the invention is simple does not deny it patentability.

The *Windsurfer* test

The clearest modern test for determining the presence of an inventive step is the Court of Appeal's judgment in *Windsurfing International v Tabur Marine (Great Britain)* (1985), involving the navigable boom for a windsurfer.

Figure 3.5

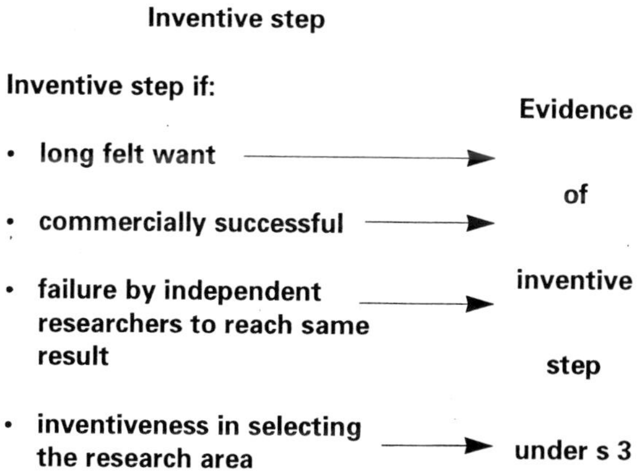

Inventive step

Inventive step if:

Evidence

* **long felt want** ——————▶

of

* **commercially successful** —————▶

inventive

* **failure by independent** ————▶
  researchers to reach same
  result

step

* **inventiveness in selecting** —————▶ **under s 3**
  the research area

The court proposed a four-fold test:

(a) identifying the inventive concept in the patent;

(b) imputing to the normally skilled, but imaginative addressee what was common general knowledge in the state of the art;

(c) identifying the differences, if any, between the matter cited and the alleged invention;

(d) deciding whether those differences, without the benefit of hindsight, would have amounted to steps that the skilled address would take, or whether an inventive step was necessary.

Figure 3.6

STEPS IN *WINDSURFER* (1985)

Inventive concept

↓

Common general knowledge

↓

Differences between invention and general knowledge

↓

Were differences obvious or would a mental leap be necessary?

In *Molynycke AB v Proctor & Gamble Ltd* (1992), the *Windsurfer* principles were restated as follows:

(a) What is the inventive step?

(b) What was the state of the art at the priority date?

(c) In what respect does the step go beyond or differ from the state of the art?

(d) Would the step be obvious to a skilled man?

Industrial application

An invention must be of industrial application, ie, there must be a vendible product or way of achieving the process. For example, a machine that make can make rain from fog has been held to produce a vendible product (*Elton and Leda Chemicals* (1957)).

But a scheme for laying new pipes and cables to minimise disruption to roads (*Hillier's Application* (1969)) does not involve industrial application, there being no vendible product.

Procedure for applying for a patent

A patent can be obtained through either the British Patent Office or the European Patent Office, the latter being treated as if the applicant had obtained it through the UK Office.

Applications must be in English (*Rhode and Schwarz's Application* (1980)) and fulfil the requirements of s 14(2) of the PA 1977.

The application must be made by the inventor or joint inventor (s 7(2)(a) of the PA 1977).

The crucial document for an applicant is the specification in which the invention must be clearly disclosed sufficiently for it to be performed by a person skilled in the art (ss 14(3) of the PA 1977). The language must be clear enough to enable another person to be able to use the invention once the patent expires (*Edison and Swan United Electric Co v Holland* (1889)).

The specification consists of two parts:

(a) the description (which may include diagrams and technical drawings) explaining how the invention works and usually the abstract;

(b) the claims which cover the scope of the legal monopoly claimed by the patentee.

The wording of the claims is crucial and words and phraseology fall to be construed according to general and specific rules of interpretation.

There is no requirement to describe every possible way in which the invention is to be utilised (*Quantel Ltd v Spaceward Microsystems Ltd* (1990)).

Filing

When completed, the application must be filed with the Patent Office, under s 5(1) of the PA 1977. The priority date of the invention is the date upon which the application is filed at the Patent Office.

Preliminary examination and search

Section 17 is concerned with preliminary examination and search which has to be done before publication.

Publication

Within 18 months, the application must be published by the Patent Office allowing public inspection of the applicant's claim, as required by s 16(1).

Substantial examination and search

Within six months after publication, the applicant should request an examination and search.

The examination ensures that the patent fulfils the requirements of patentability under s 1(1).

The examiner investigates the application to the extent considered necessary (s 17(4)) and any objections to patentability must be raised with the applicant. Arguments must be made within four years and six months from the initial application, unless an appeal to the Patents Court is pending.

As soon as is practicable after a patent has been granted, the Comptroller must publish a notice in the Official Journal of Patents that the patent has been granted; a certificate is issued to the applicant. The effect of the grant puts an end to all pre-grant procedures (*ITT Industries Inc's Application* (1984)).

Figure 3.7

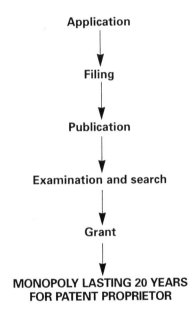

STEPS IN OBTAINING A PATENT

Application

↓

Filing

↓

Publication

↓

Examination and search

↓

Grant

↓

**MONOPOLY LASTING 20 YEARS
FOR PATENT PROPRIETOR**

Once granted, the patent provides a monopoly for the proprietor of the patent in the invention concerned.

Infringement proceedings

The use or dealing with a patented invention without the permission of the proprietor will be an infringement and the proprietor of the patent will be entitled to take action through the courts to protect his monopoly.

To amount to an infringement the defendant must do an act which comes within the claims in the patent.

The earliest date that an infringement can occur is the date on which the application is published, normally 18 months after the priority date. But such an infringement is not actionable until the patent is granted.

Infringement of the patent consists of any of the following acts done without the consent of the proprietor of the patent, as set out in s 60 of the PA 1977:

(a) making, disposing of, offering to dispose of, importing, using or keeping a patented product;

(b) using a patented process or offering for use in the UK;

(c) disposing of, offering to dispose of, using or importing any product obtained by using a process or keeping such a product.

'Offering to dispose' was considered in *Kalman v PCL Packaging* (1982), where it was held that disposal must include selling of an article.

Keeping a product was considered in *Smith Kline and French v Harbottle* (1980), where it was taken as meaning 'keeping in stock' for sale, rather than acting simply as a 'mere custodian or warehouseman'.

Innocent infringement will be as much an infringement as a deliberate one (*Wilbec Plastics Ltd v Wilson Dawes Ltd* (1966)).

Figure 3.8

INFRINGING ACTS

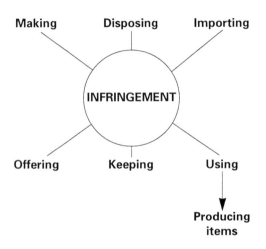

Defences for patent infringement

A variety of defences may exist to a claim of patent infringement.

Acts which do and do not amount to infringements are set out in s 60(5)(a)–(f).

Accidental infringement

An accidental infringement, eg, where a product is manufactured by accident, will not amount to an infringement.

Private use

Acts done privately or for non-commercial purposes are not infringements (s 60(5)(a) of the PA 1977).

Experiments

Acts done for experimental purposes relating to the subject matter of the patent will not be infringements.

Prior use

A prior user of an invention will have a defence (s 64 of the PA 1977).

Lack of title

A defence can be raised on the basis that patent holder has been wrongly granted the patent and should never have obtained title.

Licence

A defendant may claim a licence to do the acts complained of by the patentee. A licence may be express or implied and may be granted orally or in writing.

Repair

A licence to repair an item may be implied where a purchaser gives a third party an item to repair.

Whether a repair has taken place is a question of fact – a new item should not be made under the guise of repair (*Solar Thompson Engineering v Barton* (1977)).

Exhaustion of rights

Section 60(4) of the PA 1977 will implement the doctrine of the exhaustion of disposal rights where a product has been put on the market with the consent of the proprietor of the patent. Where a proprietor has agreed to one disposal of a product he is debarred from objecting from subsequent disposals.

It does not apply to goods imported from non-EC countries where there is no licence.

Frequently, a defendant in a patent suit may defend the proceedings by a so called 'Gillette defence'. This arose from the case of *Gillette v Anglo American Trading* (1913), where the defendant claimed that the plaintiff's patent was invalid because he was doing what the plaintiff was doing before the plaintiff filed the patent application. Claims that a patent fails for lack of novelty or inventive step are frequently raised by defendants in infringement proceedings.

Revocation of a patent

A patent may be revoked under s 72 of the PA 1977.

Grounds for revocation are:

(a) the invention is not a patentable invention;

(b) the patent was granted to a person who was not entitled to be granted that patent;

(c) the specification of the patent does not disclose it sufficiently;

(d) unallowable amendments.

Applications must normally be commenced within two years of the grant of the patent, except in cases where the registered proprietor knew he was not entitled to the grant.

These provisions do not affect revocation being sought during civil proceedings or the right of the Comptroller to revoke a patent (s 72(5) and s 73 proceedings).

Construction of patent claims

Construction of patent claims is important for the patentee as it defines the scope of the monopoly and for others who wish to make or use similar items. Where an identical product is produced or manufactured without licence, infringement is clearly established, but problems arise when an alleged infringer produces a variant of the invention.

Here, the court has to determine whether the invention has been copied in a way which infringes the claims of the patent monopoly

The patent must be described so as to make it clear in respect of what the patent is granted.

From *Clark v Addie* (1877), the courts developed the 'pith and marrow' doctrine that the patent might be applied to parts of an invention (known as integers).

The pith and marrow doctrine sought to determine situations where the court considered the essential integers had been copied.

However, since the case of *Catnic Components Ltd v Hill and Smith* (1982), the courts have followed what has been termed the 'purposive approach' of examining the purpose underlying the integers in an invention, rather than applying a literal approach to interpreting the claims of a patent.

The purposive approach that was followed in *Improver Corp v Remington Consumer Products Ltd* (1990) developed three '*Catnic* questions' to determine the width of a patent monopoly:

(a) Does the variant put forward have a material effect upon the way in which the invention works ?

If yes, the invention is outside the claim and does not infringe.

(b) If no, would the variant have been obvious to a reader skilled in the art?

If no, it is outside the claim.

(c) If yes, would a reader skilled in the art understand that the patentee expected strict compliance as an essential requirement of the invention?

If yes, the variant is outside the claim.

Determining ownership

Section 7 provides that any person may apply for a patent, individually or jointly. Under s 7(2), a patent may be granted to the inventor or joint inventors or to any other person entitled by operation of law.

Section 7(3) states that the inventor is the person who devised the invention.

Section 7(2)(b) provides that a person entitled to the property in the patent can make a claim.

Property is owned as personal property (s 32 of the PA 1977) and may be leased, mortgaged, licensed, given away or passed by succession.

Employee inventions

Where an employee in the course of his employment has made an invention which it was part of his duty to make, the invention and, hence, the patent, belong to the employer.

Employers may obtain the benefit of a patent invented by an employee by:

(a)   contractual terms;

(b)   operation of equity or implied term (*Triplex Safety Glass v Scorah* (1938));

(c)   operation of s 39 of the PA 1977.

The court will take the approach laid down in *Harris' Patent* (1985) to determining ownership.

Section 39 of the PA 1977

Under s 39(1), inventions made by an employee in the course of employment belong to the employer where an invention is made:

(a)   in the normal course of the normal duties; or

(b)   during the course of duties where the employee was under an obligation to further his employer's interests.

With s 39(1)(a) and the normal duties of the employee, the court considers whether the employee expected to invent. (The court looks at the duties the employee is engaged to do and decides whether an invention might reasonably be expected to result.)

With s 39(1)(b), in the course of duties falling outside normal duties, the court considers whether the employee was under a special obligation to further his employer's interests at the time.

In any other situation, s 39(2) provides that the invention belongs to the employee.

The duties of the employee and the place of invention may have a crucial effect on determining the ownership of the patent (see *Electrolux Ltd v Hudson* (1977): invention made at home by employee not employed to invent; employee entitled to patent).

In *Harris' Patent* (1985), the circumstances of the duty to invent under s 39(1)(a) referred to the invention in suit, not any invention. If an invention arises from circumstances in s 39(1)(a), it will automatically fulfil the requirement of s 39(1)(b).

In *Glasgow Health Board's Application* (1996), the court had to determine ownership of an invention made by an employee with clinical responsibilities, but no contract to conduct research. The court found that the duty to treat patients did not extend to devising new devices so to do, so the application would proceed in the name of the employee alone.

Provision also exists for compensation for employees under ss 40–42 of the PA 1977, on application in prescribed situations where the benefit of the patent might otherwise go wholly to the employer.

Figure 3.9

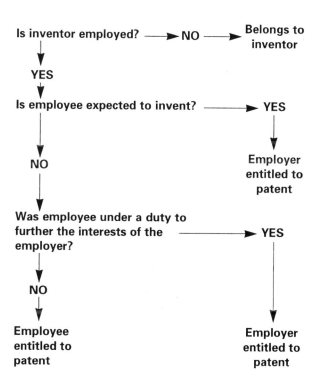

OWNERSHIP OF PATENT (s 39)

Is inventor employed? ⟶ NO ⟶ Belongs to inventor

↓ YES

Is employee expected to invent? ⟶ YES

↓ NO ↓

Employer entitled to patent

Was employee under a duty to further the interests of the employer? ⟶ YES

↓ NO ↓

Employee entitled to patent

Employer entitled to patent

INTELLECTUAL PROPERTY LAW

Damages in patent actions

Damages in patent actions may be assessed in a number of ways.

One factor is whether the plaintiff would have manufactured his or her invention or process, or would have granted licences to third parties (*Pneumatic Tyre Co v Puncture Proof Pneumatic Tyre Co* (1899)).

The court may take into consideration the number of infringing articles and multiply by the sum payable under a licence (*Meters Ltd v Metropolitan Gas Meters* (1911)).

In *Watson Laidlow & Co v Pott Cassells & Williamson* (1914), the court held that the measure of damages was the amount of profit that the plaintiff could have made minus the sales obtained by the defendant.

In *Catnic Components v Hill & Smith* (1983), the plaintiff was awarded the loss of manufacturing profits on the assumption that most of the sales of the disputed lintels would have been made by them, but not when lintels were sold in mixed packages with other products.

Remedies

Remedies in a patent infringement case are injunctions, declarations and damages, with account of profits in the alternative.

If a defendant can prove that he was not aware and had no reasonable grounds for supposing that a patent existed, then neither account of profits nor damages will be available.

Injunctions may be used to restrain potential or actual infringements (*Shoe Machinery & Co Ltd v Cutlan* (1896)).

In determining the size of awards of damages, the courts may calculate the loss in terms of the number of infringing items and the sum which would have been paid as a royalty or licence fee to the plaintiff to make the manufacture of the article lawful.

In *Gerber Garment Technology v Lectra Systems* (1995), the scope for awards of damages was extended to allow the plaintiff to recover manufacturing and marketing costs and the costs on each infringing item.

4 Copyright

UK law copyright is governed by Pt 1 of the Copyright, Designs and Patents Act 1988 (CDPA), as amended.

The Copyright Acts of 1911 and 1956 continue to be of limited effect in certain specific instances set out in the schedules to the CDPA 1988

International agreements

The CDPA 1988 must also be seen in the context of Directives from the EC and a number of important international agreements.

The most significant of these are:

The Berne Convention
This protects the rights of authors of literary and artistic works, giving owners of rights in one Convention country the same as those in another.

The Rome Convention
This affords national protection to performers, record producers and broadcasting organisations.

The Universal Copyright Convention 1952
This adopted the © symbol indicating copyright protection.

The nature of copyright protection

Copyright is essentially a negative right which prevents others from making copies of the work of an author.

Copyright is a partial monopoly and the law allows a number of exceptions whereby a work may be copied legitimately without infringing the rights of an author.

Section 1(1) of the CDPA 1988 states:

> Copyright is a property right which subsists in accordance with this Part in the following descriptions of work:
> (a) original literary, dramatic, musical or artistic works;
> (b) sound recordings, films, broadcasts or cable programmes;
> (c) the typographical arrangements of published editions.

Copyright subsistence

Copyright does not subsist in a work unless it has been:

(a) created by a qualifying person;

(b) first published in a qualifying country; or

(c) transmitted from a qualifying country.

For literary works, the work must be reduced to a material form in writing or otherwise (s 3(2)).

Figure 4.1

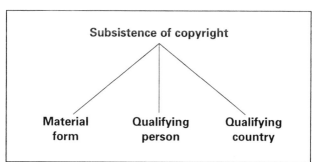

Copyright does not exist in a pure idea (*Green v New Zealand Broadcasting Corp* (1989)). The recording need not be with the permission of the author in order for the copyright to come into being. Recording can produce two separate copyrights, as in *Walter v Lane* (1900), in which a reported speech was both copyright of the speaker and the newspaper journalist who wrote it down.

A work will qualify for copyright protection if it is published in the UK or in a country to which the Act extends (s 155(1)).

Publication of a work means, under s 175(1), issuing copies of the work in question to the public. This must satisfy a reasonableness test (s 175(5)).

If a work is sold and distributed free, that is sufficient to constitute issue to the public (*British Northrop Ltd v Texteam Blackburn Ltd* (1974)). But a mere exposure or a distribution to a small class of recipients will be insufficient (*Infabrics Ltd v Jaytex Shirt Co Ltd* (1980)).

The public performance of a literary, dramatic or musical work is not publication (s 175(4)(a)(i)). Nor is an artistic work published by virtue of it being exhibited.

Originality

In order to be protected, a work must fulfil the requirement of s 1 of originality. This is in the sense that the work must 'originate' from an author as its source and creator (ie, it is not copied).

In the case of *University of London Press Ltd v University Tutorial Press* (1916), it was stated:

> ... the word original does not in this connection mean that the work must be the expression of inventive or original thought ... but that it should originate from the author.

In *Macmillan v Cooper* (1923), it was held that there was no need for an author 'to impart to the product some quality or character which the raw material did not possess' – a compilation of pre-existing works will still attract copyright. However, if no more than trifling additions and corrections are made to an existing work, it will not be sufficient to attract copyright protection anew (*Hedderwick v Griffin* (1841); *Thomas v Turner* (1886)); nor will a mere reprint of the earlier work (*Hogg v Toye & Co* (1935)).

Nonetheless, some work, skill or effort is required, even if subject matter is mundane or banal (see *Independent Television Publications v Time Out* (1984)).

If the work is not entirely novel to an author, then the question will be whether or not sufficient embellishment has been made in order to produce a new work.

In *Ibcos Computers Ltd v Barclays Mercantile Highland Finance* (1994), Jacob J stated that a fresh copyright could arise each time a modification to a computer program was made. The issue was not affected by the fact that an original work embodied elements that could only be achieved in a number of ways.

Figure 4.2

COPYRIGHT

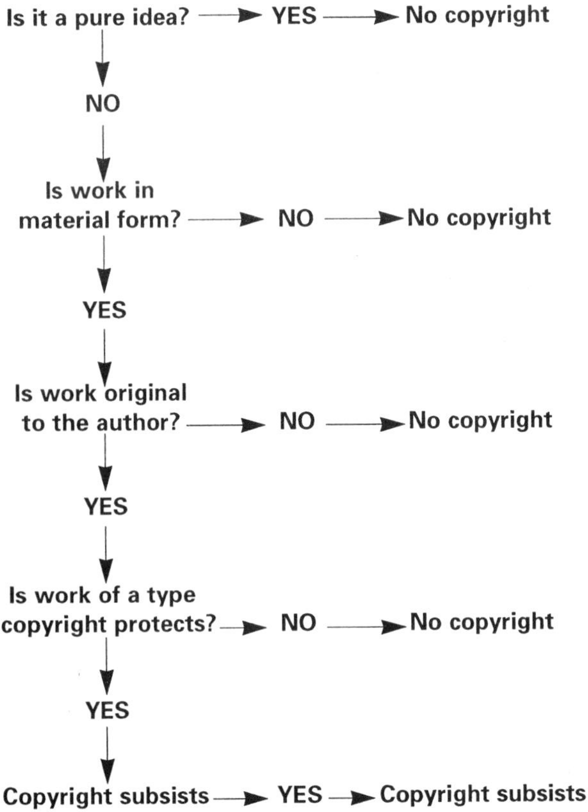

Is it a pure idea? ⟶ YES ⟶ No copyright

↓

NO

↓

Is work in material form? ⟶ NO ⟶ No copyright

↓

YES

↓

Is work original to the author? ⟶ NO ⟶ No copyright

↓

YES

↓

Is work of a type copyright protects? ⟶ NO ⟶ No copyright

↓

YES

↓

Copyright subsists ⟶ YES ⟶ Copyright subsists

No copyright exists in ideas

No copyright exists in ideas or in very simple images –
Kenrick v Lawrence (1890).

Note, however, the decision in *Mirage Productions v Counter-
Feat Clothing* (1991), but remember, this was an interlocutory
decision.

No copyright exists in news until the subject matter is
recorded in material work (*Walter v Steinkopff* (1892)).

No copyright exists in historical incidents or themes
(*Harman Pictures NV v Osborne* (1967)).

It should be recognised that it is not the *information*, but the
expression thereof which attracts copyright protection.

Figure 4.3

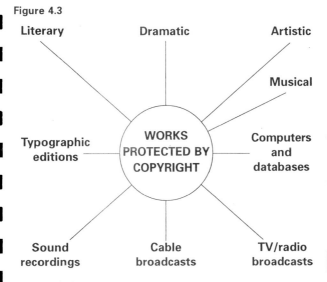

Figure 4.4

COPYRIGHT PROTECTS	COPYRIGHT DOES NOT PROTECT
✔ Original works (not copied)	✗ Ideas, plots subject matter
✔ Labour skill and effort of author	✗ News
	✗ Very simple works
✔ The expression of information by author	✗ Information itself

AUTHOR'S SOURCE MATERIAL

Originality:

Fresh labour,
skill and effort
of author
present?

↓

If YES,
an original work

Primary works

Section 3 covers literary, dramatic and musical works, as follows:

> ... 'literary work' means any work, other than a dramatic or musical work, which is written, spoken or sung and accordingly includes:
>
> (a) a table or compilation; and
>
> (b) a computer program;
>
> 'dramatic work' includes a work of dance or mime; and
>
> 'musical work' means a work consisting of music, exclusive of any words or action intended to be sung, spoken or performed with the music.

Original literary works (s 3) covers literary works which are written, spoken or sung and excludes dramatic or musical works. Literary works include tables and compilations, computer programs and preparatory design material. See also the Copyright (Computer Programs) Regulations 1992 on computer programs. Under the Copyright Act 1956 and s 1 of the Copyright (Computer Software) Amendment Act 1985, a computer program was considered a literary work and proceedings would lie to prevent reproduction of the program in a machine readable form (see *Thrustcode Computing (WW) Computing* (1983)).

Literary works

The majority of reported copyright cases have involved literary works of one description or another.

The CDPA 1988 uses the word 'work' which requires the creation to have involved labour, skill and effort.

There is no requirement for a work to have literary merit in the sense of being aesthetically pleasing, pleasurable, entertaining, educational or contributing to the common good (*Exxon Corp v Exxon Insurance* (1982)).

The concept of a literary work in the copyright context is a wide one and has been held to include compilations. Article 2.5 of the Berne Convention requires the exercise of skill in the selection of materials in a compilation.

However, UK law is flexible – copyright protection will subsist in telephone directories; lists of broadcasts and transmissions (see, eg, *BBC and ITP v Time Out* (1984)). Effort and labour is involved even though subject matter is mundane.

Examples

Private letters: *British Oxygen v Liquid Air* (1925); *Donoghue v Allied Newspapers Ltd* (1938).

Examination papers: *University of London v London Tutorial Press* (1916).

List of starting prices for horse races: *Odhams Press Ltd v London and Provincial Sporting News Agency* (1936).

Lists of football matches: *Football League Ltd v Littlewoods Pools Ltd* (1959).

A trade catalogue: *Collis v Cater* (1898).

Notes taken by a student in a lecture will attract copyright protection. There may be copyright in notes made on a non-copyright text if knowledge, skill and taste are exercised in their preparation, notwithstanding the same material is to be found in standard texts or that the notes consist of quotations from non-copyright sources: *Moffat v Gill* (1901).

Literary efforts denied copyright protection include:

- single invented words (*Exxon Corporation v Exxon Insurance Ltd* (1982));

- titles (*Francis Day & Hunter v Twentieth Century Fox Corporation Ltd* (1940) 'Man who broke the bank in Monte Carlo'; *Rose v Information Services Ltd* (1987));

- telegraph codes (*Anderson v Lieber Code* (1917));

- four commonplace sentences (*Kirk v Fleming* (1928)).

Dramatic works

A dramatic work must be capable of being performed (*Green v Broadcasting Corp of New Zealand* (1989)). It can include a work of dance or mime, as distinct from a musical work and must be recorded in writing or some other form by s 3(2) (see above).

The detailed plot of a dramatic work can be protected (*Vane v Famous Players* (1923–28)).

Artistic works

An artistic work is defined under s 4 as including:

(1) (a) a graphic work, photograph, sculpture or collage, irrespective of artistic merit;

(b) a work of architecture being a building or a model for a building;

(c) a work of artistic craftsmanship.

(2) In this Part, 'building' means any fixed structure, and a part of a building or a fixed structure.

Graphic work includes:

(a) any painting, drawing, diagram, map chart or plan;

(b) any engraving, etching, lithograph, woodcut or similar work.

'Photograph' means a recording of light or other radiation on any medium on which an image is produced or from which an image may be by any means produced which is not part of a film.

'Sculpture' includes a cast or model. Jewellery would fall into this category.

Artistic craftsmanship is covered (see *Hensher (George) v Restawhile Upholstery (Lancs)* (1976)).

In *British Leyland v Armstrong* (1986), concerning the manufacture of exhaust pipes, the co-ordinates of a pipe could be included in the definition of artistic work. To prevent monopolies based on copyright in common industrial shapes, copyright protection has been removed for articles lacking artistic merit where copying takes the form of making an article to a design or copying an article made to a design (s 51 of the CDPA 1988).

Copyright has been held to subsist in three simple circles (*Solar Thompson Engineering Co Ltd v Barton* (1977)).

Artistic works lacking permanence may not be the subject of copyright protection (*Merchandising Corp of America v*

Harpbond (1983), concerning the face paint of Adam Ant, the musician).

Architectural works and models
An architectural plan falls to be protected under s 4.

Musical works
Musical works are judged by the effect on the ear (*Austin v Columbia Gramophone Co Ltd* (1917–23)).

Under the CDPA 1988, a musical work is one consisting exclusively of musical notes, regardless of any words or actions intended to be sung, spoken or performed with it (ss 1(1)(a), 2(1)).

A separate copyright will exist in the words of a song as a literary work as well as the notes of the music as a musical work (*Redwood Music v B Feldman & Co Ltd* (1979)).

Sound recordings
Sound recordings consist of reproducible recordings of sounds, or literary, dramatic and musical works (s 5(1)) from which sounds reproducing the work or part of it may be produced.

No copyright will subsist in a sound recording that is itself a copy of another recording.

Duration of copyright in sound recordings is to the end of 50 years from the making or release of the recording.

Computer programs
Computer programs are treated as the equivalent of literary works (*Thrustcode LTD v WW Computing Ltd* (1983)), enacted into law by the Copyright (Computer Software) Act 1985.

Computer programs are specifically protected by s 3(1)(b) of the CDPA 1988, with preparatory designs protected under s 3(1)(c).

The Copyright (Computer Programs) Regulations 1992 came into effect on 1 January 1993, amending the CDPA 1988, and applies to computer programs whenever created, following EC Directive 91/250/EEC. Regulation 4 inserts new ss 50A, 50B and 50C into the CDPA 1988.

Films

'Film' means a recording on any medium (including celluloid, video and digital recording) providing a moving picture can be produced from it (s 5B(1) of the CDPA 1988).

Under the 1911 Act, films were only protected as dramatic works or a series of photographs (Sched 1, para 7 of the CPDA 1988). The 1956 Act protected films made after 1 June 1957. The CPDA 1988 applies to films made after 1 August 1989. The producer and principal director are taken to be the author (s 9(2) of the 1988 Act, substituted by SI 1997/2967). All films are protected for 70 years after the death of the principal director, screenplay author, dialogue author and music composer (duration regulations (SI 1995/3297)). For pre-1956 films, the increased term applies to dramatic or photographic copyright.

Protection has been extended for up to 70 years from the death of persons connected with the film under the directive.

Typographical editions

Under s 8, the typographical arrangement of published editions and any part thereof are protected for literary, dramatic or musical works, unless it is a reproduction of a previous typographical arrangement.

Anonymous and pseudonymous works

Works with no identifiable author are subject to protection by virtue of s 12 of the CDPA 1988.

A literary, dramatic, musical or artistic work which is anonymous or published under a pseudonym enjoys copyright protection either seventy years from the date it was made or seventy years from when it was made available to the public (Art 1(3) of the Duration Directive).

Crown and parliamentary copyright

The Crown and Parliament have copyright in works made by officials and servants in the course of their duties.

Crown copyright lasts for 50 years from publication or 125 years from creation. Parliamentary copyright only lasts for 50 years from the making.

What is protected

Copyright protects the original skill, labour and effort of an author (*Ladbroke (Football) Ltd v William Hill* (1964)).

It is not the information itself but the use that the author has made of it in the creation of an original work.

If a person has unfairly appropriated the labour, skill or effort of an author by either copying an original work or a substantial part of one, an action will lie against the infringer.

Determining whether a person has made an unfair appropriation of the work of another is considered in terms of what use the person copying has made of the work and whether he has brought fresh labour, skill and effort to the material so as to create a new original work.

In *Elanco Products v Mandops (Agrochemical Specialists) Ltd* (1979), the plaintiffs had invented a herbicide, the patent of which had expired. The herbicide was sold with a accompanying leaflet. Buckley LJ held that the defendants were entitled to make use of information that was in the public domain but not to appropriate the plaintiff's skill and judgement, thus saving the cost of time and effort in acquiring their own data.

The quality not quantity divide

The amount of the copyright work which can be taken before infringement arises is generally quite small.

In determining whether the amount of a work which has been taken amounts to a copyright infringement, the courts have stressed that the test is more one of 'quality than quantity'.

In *Ladbroke Football Ltd v William Hill* (1964), Lord Reid stated: 'the question whether the defendant has copied a substantial part depends much more on the quality than the quantity of what he has taken.'

The same view was taken in *EMI v Papathanasiou* (1987) ('*Chariots of Fire*'), where the test was taken to be qualitative not quantitative – although quantity may betray quality (*LB Plastics v Swish Products* (1979)). Copying a small part of an original work could constitute infringement.

The classic enunciation of this principle was in *University of London Press v London Tutorial Press* (1916): 'what is worth copying is worth protecting,' but this is arguably too broad, and the modern approach of the courts is to have regard to the word 'substantial' in s 16(2) of the CDPA 1988.

Figure 4.5

PROTECTED BY COPYRIGHT

Author's:

✔ **labour**

✔ **skill**

✔ **effort**

Quality not quantity

(*Ladbrooke Football Ltd v William Hill* (1964))

In *Spelling Goldberg Productions Inc v BPC Publishing Ltd* (1981), it was held that a tiny proportion of a work could be substantial if possessing a key feature by which the whole work could be identified or recognised.

The courts do not apply a percentage basis when determining when there has been appropriation. Attempts to identify a percentage basis of an amount that may be taken are notoriously unreliable – each case will turn on its facts.

In *Sillitoe v McGraw Hill Books* (1983), 5% of a novel was a substantial appropriation.

In *Express Newspapers v Liverpool Daily Post and Echo plc* (1985), one 700th of a literary work was substantial.

In *Chapple v Thompson Magazines* (1928–35), four lines of a popular song were held not to be substantial.

However, note *Kipling v Genostan* (1917–22), where four lines of the famous poem, 'If', were held to be substantial.

In *Hawkes v Paramount Films* (1934), 28 bars of 'Colonel Bogey' were held to be substantial.

Common sources

Copyright can be obtained in a work based upon common non-copyright sources which are in the public domain (*Pike v Nicholas* (1867).

In *ITP Ltd and BBC Ltd v Time Out* (1984), Whitford J stated:

> Anyone reading a copyright work based upon publicly available information is of course free to go away and starting with the public source and from that source, to produce his own work which may correspond very closely with the work of the earlier author. What he is not entitled to do is take a short cut.

It will be a legitimate use of a text to use it as a guide to non-copyright sources (*Moffat and Paige Ltd v George Gill and Sons Ltd* (1901)).

Unoriginal parts of a book, derived from non-copyright sources, may sometimes be copied without infringement arising (*Warwick Films v Eisenger* (1969)).

Reproduction of a non-fiction work as fiction

Reproductions of works dealing with factual or historic subjects reproduced in fictional form can be an infringement if a substantial part is taken (*Harman Pictures v Osborne* (1967)).

Attempts to apply a percentage basis are unreliable (*Ravenscroft v Herbert* (1980)).

Extent of alteration

The extent of alteration may be relevant in determining infringement.

Separate copyrights will not arise where only trivial corrections or alterations are made to an existing work (*Hedderwick v Griffin* (1841); *Thomas v Turner* (1886)).

An unlawful reproduction does not become less of an infringement 'because the reproducer has disfigured his reproduction with ignorant or foolish additions of his own' (*Caird v Simes* (1887)).

It is possible for a work to be infringing and original (*ZYX Music v King* (1995)).

The question is not simply whether a defendant has added a sufficient degree of skill or labour to create an original work, rather it is the use that has been made of the plaintiff's copyright work.

Determining infringement

The approach of the courts is to take a three stage test:

(a) Has copying occurred?

(b) What is substantial?

(c) Was what has been taken original ?

Figure 4.6

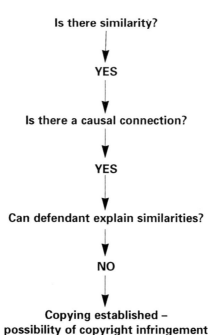

COPYING

Is there similarity?

↓

YES

↓

Is there a causal connection?

↓

YES

↓

Can defendant explain similarities?

↓

NO

↓

Copying established –
possibility of copyright infringement

Figure 4.7

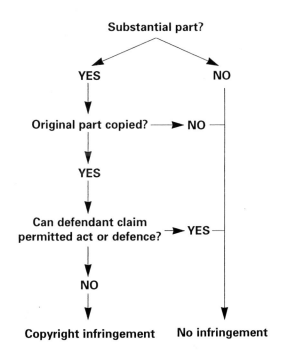

COPYING ESTABLISHED

Presumptions in copyright infringement

In an action for infringement of a literary, dramatic, musical or artistic work, it is presumed:

(a) that the person who is named as author is the author;

(b) that if first publication of a work qualifies it for copyright, copyright subsists and was owned at first publication by the person named as publisher;

(c) that where the author is dead or unidentifiable when the action is brought, the work was original and was first published at the date the plaintiff alleges (s 104).

Figure 4.8

PRESUMPTIONS

Named author	=	**author**
OR		
First publisher	=	**owner of copyright**
Dead or anonymous author	=	**work is original and published at date stated**

Infringement

Tests for copying

It should be recognised that there is no tort of copying – it is where the copyright is infringed that liability arises in law.

The approach of the courts is to examine the two works for similarities. If similarity is revealed between the two works, the burden of proof then shifts to the defendant to explain away the similarities (*Corelli v Gray* (1913)).

Liability arises whether copying is deliberate or unconscious (*Francis Day Hunter v Bron* (1963)).

Indirect copying will equally be an infringement of an original work (*Purefoy v Sykes Boxall* (1954)).

A reproduction of a work changing the scale of dimensions of a work may be an infringement.

A causal connection must be shown between the two works (*Francis Day Hunter v Bron* (1963)).

In *Billhofer Maschinenfabrik GmbH v TH Dixon & Co Ltd* (1990), it was said, obiter, that when considering causal connection as to whether an alleged infringement was copied from a copyright work, it was the resemblance in essentials, the small, redundant, even mistaken elements of a copyright work which carried the greatest weight, because these were the least likely to have arisen through independent design.

With very simple drawings, the degree of similarity must be very close (*Politechnika Ipari Szovetkezet v Dallas Print Transfers Ltd* (1982)).

Literary works

Copyright in a book can be infringed where an undue amount of material is used, even if the language is different or the text is 'scrambled' (*Chatterton v Cave* (1878); *Elanco Products Ltd v Mandops (Agrochemical Specialists) Ltd* (1980)). Again, what is protected is the labour, work, skill and effort of the author.

Artistic works

In cases involving artistic works, the courts have looked to the resemblance to the original and whether what is copied is a significant part.

There is no copyright in artistic themes (*Baumann v Fussell* (1978)).

In *West v Francis* (1822), the courts stated: 'a copy is that which comes so near to the original as to give every person seeing it the idea created by the original.'

In *Spectravest Inc v Aperknit Ltd* (1988), similarity in artistic work was judged by the impression on the eye.

With a number of similar drawings of one image or character, eg, cartoon characters, the court may look at points of similarity.

Examples

King Features Syndicate v Kleeman (1941) ('Popeye').

Mirage Studios v Counter Feat Clothing Co Ltd (1991) ('Ninja Turtles') even if it is not possible to prove that a particular image has been copied.

Musical works

Copying of musical works is judged by the effect on the ear.

In *Stephenson v Chappell & Co Ltd* (1935), the use of identical notes constituting the melody in two songs was *prima facie* evidence of infringement.

Dramatic works

Dramatic works will not be infringed if only the bare plot has been copied (*Sutton Vane Famous Players* (1928–35), and there will be no infringement in standard or stock scenes, since these will lack the originality of the first work (see *Dagnall v British and Dominion Film Corps Co Ltd* (1928–35)). It is an infringement to transform a non-dramatic work into a dramatic one (eg, turning an autobiographical work into a drama without permission), and vice versa, under s 21(3)(a)(ii).

Infringement of computer programs

In *Ibcos Computers Ltd v Barclays Mercantile Highland Finance* (1994), the court considered claims by a plaintiff that copyright subsisted in:

(a) individual programs and sub-routines;

(b) the general structure of the software;

(c) certain general design features of the software defined in expert reports adduced by the plaintiff.

Jacob J held that the approach to be taken was:

(a) whether copyright subsisted in the relevant works;

(b) whether there had been copying;

(c) whether substantial copying had taken place – by comparison.

Proving copying requires:

(a) the defendant had access to the program;

(b) similarities between the works

In *MS Associates v Power* (1985), it was held that, if there is only one way of expressing information, infringement may not be taken as occurring.

It will not be an infringement of a computer program to make a back-up copy (Art 5(2) of the Software Directive;

s 50A of the CDPA 1988). Section 50B covers decompilations and, s 50C, lawful users.

Screen displays may be protected as artistic works (*Atari v Phillips* (1995)).

Copying

Copyright in a work is infringed by copying the work, issuing copies of it to the public, or making an adaptation of it without licence (ss 16–18).

Reproduction in any material form will amount to an infringement of copyright (s 17).

These include:

(a) storing by electronic means – eg, computers;

(b) converting a two dimensional work into three dimensions and a three dimensional work into two dimensions.

Under s 17(6), transient or incidental copies are infringements.

Adaptation

Section 21 of the CDPA 1988 provides that an adaptation of a literary work (with the exception of a computer program), without permission, may be an infringement. Under s 21(3), an adaptation includes:

(a) a translation;

(b) a version of a dramatic work when changed into a non-dramatic one or vice versa;

(c) a version of the work conveyed by pictures.

Databases

Database protection is harmonised amongst EC Member States by the Directive on the Protection of Databases (March 1996).

Rights of the author of a copyright work

If material is entitled to protection, the right vested in the copyright owner is that of preventing others from doing certain specified acts, called restricted acts.

Under s 16, the author of a work enjoys exclusive rights to:

(a) copy the work;

(b) issue copies to the public;

(c) perform, show or play the work in public;

(d) broadcast the work or include it in a cable program;

(e) make an adaptation of the work or do any of the above.

Section 16(2) provides that to do any of these acts without the authority of the author is an infringement of copyright.

Section 16(3) provides that infringement arises whether the acts are done in respect of a substantial part of the work or a whole.

Strict liability applies, even if the copier believes that he is entitled to carry out the act, but innocent belief will go to the measure of any damages.

Figure 4.9

Section 16: rights of author

INFRINGEMENT – RESTRICTED ACTS

- Copying

- Issuing

- Performing

- Broadcasting

- Adapting

Authorship

The author is the person who creates the work (s 9).

This is the person whose labour, skill and effort bring the work into existence. The author must be a British citizen or subject, or domiciled or resident in the UK (s 154(4)(b)), or in a country to which the CPDA 1988 applies.

Cummins v Bond (1927): the person who holds the pen is the creator of the literary work unless he is simply writing down the dictated words of another (so called amanuensis).

Donoghue v Allied Newspapers Ltd (1938): where a ghost writer has been used, the copyright belongs to the 'ghost'.

In *Wiseman v George Weidenfield & Nicholson Ltd and Donaldson* (1985), it was held that copyright subsists with the author who puts ideas into form and development; mere supply of ideas does not generate a claim of joint ownership.

See 'Ownership' (below).

Performing and transmission

With the exception of artistic works, it is an infringement to show or perform works in public without authorisation of the copyright owner. It is also an infringement to broadcast or transmit by cable (ss 19 and 20). The Performing Rights Society protects the copyright of authors by 'policing' unauthorised performances.

As to the meaning of public performance, see *Harms (Inc) Ltd v Martans Club (Ltd)* (1926) (performance in a club as a performance in public).

See also:

- *Jennings v Stephens* (1936);
- *Turner v PRS* (1943);
- *PRS v Harlequin* (1979).

Performing rights

Performers enjoy performing rights under Pt II.

These include performances before 1 August 1989, by operation of s 180(3).

Performing rights exist in the performance of an musician, singer or acting.

Secondary infringement

Sections 22–26 of the CDPA 1988 create the concept of secondary infringement which may catch persons who knowingly enable or assist in primary infringements.

Secondary infringement occurs where a person without the licence of the owner:

- imports an infringing copy (s 22);
- possesses an infringing copy (s 23);
- sells, exhibits or distributes infringing copies (s 23);
- deals with items used for making infringing copies of specific works (s 24);
- permits premises to be used for an infringing performance (s 25);
- provides apparatus for infringing performances (s 26).

An article is defined as an infringing copy where its making is an infringement of the copyright in a work (s 27).

Knowledge is an essential element. Examples include: providing methods whereby infringing copies can be made, eg, photocopiers; providing premises for unauthorised performances, or by importing copies.

Shutting one's eyes to the obvious can be infringement (*R v Kyslant* (1934)).

Each act of infringement will be a separate tortious act.

A director may be liable for infringement by a firm (*Besson (AP) Ltd v Fulleon Ltd* (1986)).

Figure 4.10

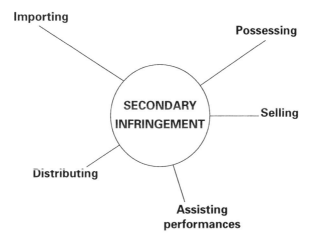

Moral rights

The CDPA 1988 provides rights of paternity and integrity and the right not to have works treated in a derogatory manner (ss 77–89).

The right to paternity: this recognises the right of the author to be identified as creator.

Figure 4.11

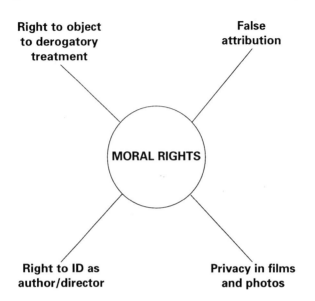

Effect of copyright protection

If material is entitled to protection, the right vested in the copyright owner is that of preventing others from doing certain specified acts, called restricted acts.

The author has exclusive rights to copy the work, issue copies to the public, perform, show or play the work in public, broadcast the work or include it in a cable programme, make an adaptation of the work or do any of the above (s 16, see above).

Strict liability applies, even if the copier believes that he is entitled to carry out the act, but innocent belief will go to the measure of any damages.

Figure 4.12

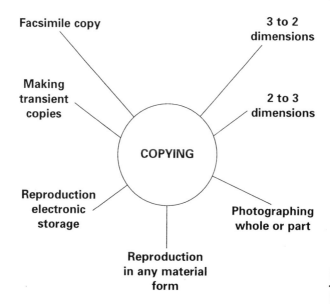

Reproduction in any material form (s 17 of the CPDA 1988)

The copying of the work is an act restricted by the copyright in every description of a copyright work.

Copying in relation to a literary, dramatic, musical or artistic work means reproducing the work in any material form (s 17(2)).

This includes reproducing a three dimensional work in two dimensions and vice versa (s 17(2)) including the storage of the work in any medium by electronic means.

Section 17 also catches the making of a photograph of the whole or any substantial part of any image forming part of a film, broadcast or cable programme and making facsimile copies of typographical arrangements.

Permitted acts

Sections 28–76 of the CDPA 1988 provide for a wide range of circumstances in which reproduction will not be an infringement. Reproduction will be lawful providing it is done for one of the permitted reasons. (Note, also, public interest, under s 171.)

Fair dealing (ss 29–30) may mean reproduction is legitimate – the court judges the fairness of the defendant's conduct.

Fair dealing may be raised where the copying of the work is for the purposes of:

(a) research and private study (s 29);

(b) criticism or review (s 30);

(c) reporting current events (excluding photographs) (s 31).

Current events can include historical matters, eg, *Associated Newspapers v News Group Newspapers* (1986).

See *Beloff v Pressdram* (1973).

In *Hubbard v Vosper* (1972), Lord Denning held that fair dealing was incapable of an all-embracing definition and each case would turn on its facts.

Denning suggested the following were all relevant:

(a) number of quotations;

(b) extent of quotations;

(c) the use made of the extracts (is there comment, criticism or review?);

(d) proportion of extracts to the amount of comment, however, each case will turn on its facts.

Figure 4.13

FAIR DEALING

- **Private study?**

- **Criticism/review?**

- **News reporting?**

- **Acknowledgment?**

- **Is use by the defendant fair?**

Short extracts from World Cup soccer games taken from BBC broadcasts and reproduced on satellite TV news broadcasts were not infringements (*British Broadcasting Corp v British Satellite Broadcasting* (1992)).

Reproduction of an entire work can conceivably amount to a fair dealing – provided that the copier is *bona fide* engaging in one of the permitted acts.

Claims of a defence of fair dealing will be scrutinised closely. In *Sillitoe v McGraw Hill Books* (1983), the defendants published extracts of books used in English literature courses in manuals for study revision. The claimed defence of fair dealing failed as the copying was for their own commercial purposes, not for those of the students who might legitimately have raised such a defence.

Figure 4.14

HOW HAS THE DEFENDANT USED THE WORK?

FAIR USES	UNFAIR USES
✔ As a guide to earlier sources	✘ To save time, labour and effort
✔ News reporting	✘ Merely reproducing
✔ Criticism or review	✘ Reproduction without acknowledgment
✔ Private research and study	✘ Exploitation or profit without licence
✔ Other permitted Act uses	✘ Malicious motive
✔ Public interest	

There is a public interest in free speech (*Kennard v Lewis* (1983)), but the claim will not automatically be a justification (*Associated Newspapers v News Group plc* (1986)).

The fair dealing defence can now only be made out where there has been a sufficient acknowledgement under s 178, the fairness being derived from the fact that the party copying is not seeking to assert rights of ownership over the work.

Acknowledgement involves the 'act of recognising the position or claims of a person' (*Sillitoe v McGraw Hill Books* (1983)).

Permitted acts

Private study or research	s 29
Criticism, review, news reporting	s 30
Incidental inclusion	s 31
Educational, libraries and archives	s 32–44
Collective licensing	s 35
Public administration	s 45–50
Judicial proceedings	s 45
Back-up copies of computer programs	s 50A
Design documents, models	s 51–52
Spoken word	s 58
Public recital	s 59
Scientific abstracts	s 60

A speaker enjoys copyright in his words under the 1988 Act.

Section 58 allows where a record of spoken words is made, in writing or otherwise, for the purposes of:

(a)   reporting current events;

(b)   broadcasting or including in a cable programme service the whole or part of a work, it is not an infringement of any copyright in the words of a literary work to use the record or material taken from it, or to copy the record, or any such material, provided certain conditions are met.

The qualifying conditions under s 58 are very important and will not justify use of a record without express permission.

Section 58(2) provides:

(i)   the record must be a direct record;

(ii) the making of the record was not prohibited by the speaker, and where copyright already existed, it did not infringe that copyright;

(iii) the record is not of a type prohibited by the speaker (so called 'off the record').

Figure 4.15

SECTION 58 OF THE CPDA

- **Direct record not prohibited**

- **No copyright infringement**

- **Not 'off the record'**

Section 51 of the CPDA 1988

Section 51 removes copyright protection from the shape or configuration of an article except where it is: (a) an artistic work in its own right; (b) a typeface.

Under Regulation 2 of the Copyright (Industrial Process and Excluded Articles (No 2) Order 1989, an industrial process is one which involved the production of more than 50 articles not forming a set.

Ownership of copyright

Section 11 of the CDPA 1988 provides that copyright normally belongs to the person who created the work – 'the author'. In the case of sound recordings and films, the author is deemed to be the person responsible for making the arrangements for the sound or film recording (s 9(2)).

Note that physical possession of the work, eg, original manuscript, photograph, etc, does not entitle one to the copyright in the work. For example, a person may leave the physical expression of an original work in their will – but this does not necessarily mean that the beneficiary will have the copyright to it (see *Re Dickens* (1935) – manuscripts written by Charles Dickens did not confer the copyright).

Section 9 is subject to s 11 of the CDPA 1988 which provides that, where a person creates a work under a contract of employment, then the ownership will lie with the employer, subject to any contractual terms in the contract of employment (with special provision for the Crown (s 11(3))).

In *Byrne v Statist* (1914), B was employed in the editorial office of *The Financial Times*. He was able to speak Portuguese and, along with two others, was asked by the paper to quote his terms for making a translation of a speech in Portuguese. B was selected for the translation, which he did in his spare time. It was held that the copyright remained with him, not with the paper because translation was not part of his normal duties.

In *Stephenson, Jordan and Harrison Ltd v MacDonald and Evans* (1952), the plaintiffs were a firm of management consultants. H and ex-employee wrote a book on management consultancy. The plaintiffs claimed to be entitled to the copyright in it, since it was based on notes prepared by H whilst assigned on duties. The Court of Appeal held that the employers were the owners of the copyright in that section of the book.

The employers were unable to assert copyright in the section of the book which was based upon three public lectures which H had given, even though the text had been typed by the plaintiffs' staff. It was held that, as H had not received extra remuneration for lecturing, lectures were not part of his duties as an employee; the court stated that the lectures represented services supplied from which the company gained publicity. Copyright vested in the employee.

In *Beloff v Pressdram* (1973), an internal memo made by the plaintiff for *The Observer* was owned by the newspaper, the issue being whether she was employed under a contract of service or a contract for services.

Where an employer surrenders copyright whether by accident or design, the agreement does not have to be in any particular form. A court may deduce the situation through general employment law principles and all the circumstances of the case.

Where an author is transferring copyright, actual or future it is necessary that there is a written document. Section 90(3) provides that an assignment of copyright is not effective unless it is in writing signed by or on behalf of the assignor.

Section 91 deals with future copyright. An agreement made in relation to future copyrights, again requires a signed instrument.

With future copyrights, the circumstances can be different on occasion, as with *AG v Guardian Newspapers* (1988). The House of Lords was prepared to accept that there could be occasions where a duty of confidence or good faith was owed and copyright could be held on a constructive equitable trust for another (ex-MI5 officer holding copyright for the Crown – the *Spycatcher* case).

Joint ownership

Joint ownership may arise through s 10(1) of the CDPA 1988. Copyright is held by joint authors where their efforts are indistinguishable. Joint authorship does not arise where a creative work is compounded of parts that demand separate distinguishable contributions, eg, in a film or play there may be separate copyrights for the script, music, scenery, costume design, etc. 'Ghost writers' writing up a celebrity's reminiscences remain owners of the copyright, not the celebrity (*Donoghue v Allied Newspapers* (1938)).

In *Levy v Rutley* (1871), it was held that co-authorship arises where collaborators work together in 'prosecution of a preconcerted joint design'.

Ownership of the copyright will be as tenants in common *Powell v Head* (1879.) Permission of both co-authors is needed to confer a licence (see *Mail Newspapers v Express Newspapers* (1987) – one author clinically dead). But one author can sue without permission of the other in case of infringement and copyright will last for 70 years after the death of the last surviving author (s 12(4) of the CDPA 1988).

It is possible to assign or licence copyrights, including future copyrights and bequeath them. Transfers must be in writing to be valid (s 92).

Duration

Copyright subsists for defined periods:

(a) literary, artistic, dramatic and musical works: 70 years from the end of the calendar year in which the author died;

(b) sound recordings and films: 50 years from the year in which they were made or released;

(c) broadcasts and cable programmes: 50 years from the end of the year in which it was first broadcast or transmitted;

(d) typographical arrangements: 25 years from the end of the calendar year in which the edition was published.

Copyright remedies

Regulated by case law and statute. Section 96 of the CDPA 1988 provides that a plaintiff is entitled to all such relief by way of damages, injunctions, account of profits or otherwise as are available in any other action involving the infringement of property rights.

Section 97 covers damages for copyright infringement and in some cases damage may be presumed.

In *Holmes v Langfier* (1903), a photographic portrait was published without permission – damage was presumed.

Innocent infringement by a defendant does not give rise to a right to damages (s 97(1) of the CDPA 1988).

Additional damages may be recoverable (s 97(2)) having regard to all the circumstances including:

(a) the flagrancy of the breach;

(b) any benefit accruing to the defendant from the infringement.

In *Nichols Advanced Systems v Rees and Oliver* (1979), Templeman J awarded damages where the defendants had received benefits and inflicted humiliation and loss and the conduct of one party had been deceitful and treacherous.

As an alternative to damages, a plaintiff may elect an account of profits and seek to recover the profits which the defendant has made through the infringement.

Statutory additional damages may be awarded whether a plaintiff elected for damages or account of profits – the award is a separate power of the court (*Cala Homes (South) Ltd and Others v Alfred McAlpine Homes East Ltd* (1996)).

Injunctions will lie for breaches of copyright, both interlocutory and final injunctions at trial.

An injunction is frequently sought on the principles discussed above, pp 1–5.

5 Passing off

The UK has no law of unfair competition but the common law tort of passing off enables a trader to protect the goodwill a business enjoys.

Goodwill is intangible – it exists in the minds of the public, thus bringing it within the ambit of intellectual property.

The goodwill must be attached to a name or 'get-up' which the plaintiff can claim belongs exclusively to him. In a sense, passing off can be described as the law protecting unregistered trade marks.

Passing off may apply in situations where trade mark protection does not apply; where a registered trade mark exists the owner may sue in passing off as well as infringement (see *Wagamama Ltd v City Centre Restaurants* (1995)).

Passing off may also be used to protect titles of books and publications which cannot be protected through copyright.

The concept of passing off is based on the principle that a trader must not 'sell his own goods under the pretence that they are the goods of another man' (*Perry v Truefitt* (1842)) and that to do so is an actionable wrong.

As it is part of the common law, the definition of passing off is open to evolution and restatement which can make a passing off action unpredictable.

However, the classic definition enunciated by Lord Parker, in *Spalding v Gamage* (1915), that 'no person is entitled to represent his goods as another's' is still applicable.

More recently, the essential elements of passing off were identified by Lord Diplock in *Erven Warnink BV v Townend & Sons (Hull) Ltd* (1979) as:

(a) a misrepresentation;

(b) made by a trader in the course of trade;

(c) to his prospective customers or ultimate consumers of goods and services supplied by him;

(d) which is calculated to injure the business or goodwill of another trade;

(e) which results in damage to the business or goodwill of the trader or which is likely to do so.

Figure 5.1

Advocaat (1979)

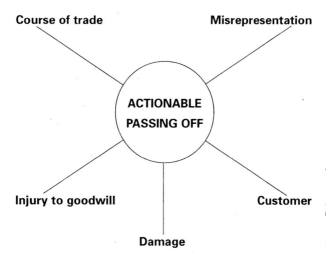

In *Reckitt and Coleman v Borden* (1990) (the *Jif Lemon* case), the definition of passing off was reduced to three elements by Lord Oliver:

(a) goodwill or reputation attached to goods and services;

(b) a misrepresentation made to the public;

(c) damage.

Figure 5.2

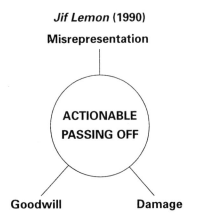

***Jif Lemon* (1990)**

Misrepresentation

ACTIONABLE PASSING OFF

Goodwill   **Damage**

The definition in *Reckitt & Coleman v Borden* (1990) has been endorsed in subsequent cases, notably *Consorzio del Proscuito di Parma v Marks & Spencer* (1991) and *Harrods v Harrodian School* (1996).

Thus, wherever a defendant adopts or uses the name or mark of another trader in such a way that customers are deceived, an action for passing off may lie. A trader may refer to a rival's name but must do so fairly.

The state of mind of the defendant is irrelevant; deception may be deliberate, negligent or innocent (*Gillette v Edenwest* (1994)). The test is whether passing off is a reasonably foreseeable consequence of the deception (the *Advocaat* case).

Get-up

The goodwill must be associated with a name or distinctive 'get-up' which acts as a badge of trade applied either to the goods or services themselves or with the name the business trades under. The name may be either real or invented (see *Hines v Winnick* (1948)).

Examples

Product name – *Bollinger v Costa Brava* (1960) ('champagne').

Advertising – *Cadbury-Schweppes Pty Ltd v Pub Squash Co Pty Ltd* (1981).

Colours – *Hoffman La Roche v DDSA Pharmaceuticals* (1968).

Packaging – *William Edge & Sons v William Nicolls* (1911) ('Dolly blue' washing powder).

Shapes – *John Haig & Co v Forth Blending Co* (1953).

Initials and combinations of letters may acquire a goodwill – see *Du Cros v Gold* (1912) and *IDW Superstores v Duncan Harris* (1975).

Titles – *Mothercare UK Ltd v Penguin Books Ltd* (1987).

In *Office Cleaning Services* it was held that in the case of trade names, the courts do not readily assume confusion between one trader and another where commonplace names or descriptive terms are used. This means that the name or get-up must be distinctive. However, with invented or fancy words, the risk of confusion and deception will be assumed much more readily.

It does not matter that the public do not know the precise identity of the trader, provided they associate the name or get-up with particular goods coming from a particular source (see, eg, *Birmingham Vinegar Brewery Co v Powell* (1897) (concerning 'Yorkshire relish')).

Goodwill

In *IRC v Muller* (1901), it was stated that 'goodwill is the attractive force which brings customers in'.

In a passing off action, it is necessary to establish that the name or get-up of the goods has acquired a reputation, and trading for a limited period may be sufficient to confer goodwill.

Goodwill may be geographically limited (*Bernadin et Cie v Pavilion Properties Ltd* (1967); *Chelsea Man v Chelsea Girl* (1987)).

It may be possible to obtain an injunction in the UK, even though the trade takes place abroad (see *Maxim's Ltd v Dye* (1978)).

Goodwill may attach to a business even if operating only for a short time (*Stannard v Reay* (1967)). On occasion, it has even been held to exist with pre-launch activities (see *Colgate Palmolive v Markwell Finance* (1989)).

Figure 5.3

GOODWILL – ATTRACTIVE FORCE BRINGING CUSTOMERS IN

Must be:

✔ associated with name or 'get up'

May be:

✔ geographically limited

✔ limited in time

The misrepresentation – who is to be deceived?

In a passing off case, it must be shown that customers or potential customers are likely to be deceived.

Any special features of target customers will be considered:

* *White v Asian Trading Organisation* (1964) (language barriers relevant);

* *William Edge & Sons v William Nicolls & Sons* (1911) (the 'Dolly blue' case: 'washerwomen, cottagers and other persons in humble station').

* *Hodgkinson & Corby Ltd v Wards Mobility* (1994) (astute health care professionals);

There is no need to prove that anyone has actually been deceived (*Bourne Swan v Edgar* (1903)).

If the defendant has set out to deceive, the law usually concludes he has succeeded (see *Slazenger v Feltham* (1889)).

Confusion

Mere confusion is normally not enough to amount to misrepresentation – it is necessary for a customer to be deceived (*Marcus Publishing v Hutton Wild* (1990)). See also *My Kinda Town (t/a Chicago Ribshack) v Dr Pepper's Store* (1983).

However, in *Chelsea Man v Chelsea Girl* (1987), it was held that damage could take a number of forms, including confusion between two businesses experienced by traders and customers.

Common field of activity

McCullough v May (1947): the claim of the plaintiff (a children's entertainer) failed as he had no common field of commercial activity with a breakfast cereal manufacturer.

In *Wombles Ltd v Wombles Skips* (1977), there was no likelihood of confusion between the owners of goodwill in children's characters and metal rubbish skips produced by the defendant.

In *Lego v Lemelstrich* (1983), although there was no common field of activity, there was a risk of damaging association and loss of licensing opportunity.

However, in recent years, there has been a retreat away from the common field of activity doctrine, as in *Harrods v Harrodian School* (1996). The Court of Appeal rejected a claim that the use of the name by the defendants at an educational establishment would cause such damage to the reputation of the well known store and that 'to be known for one thing is not the same as to be known for everything'.

Personal names

The law allows some degree of freedom for a trader to conduct business under his name, though this right has been curtailed in the 20th century:

- *Turton v Turton* (1889) (natural persons could trade under their personal names and could not be restrained);

- *Marengo v The Daily Sketch* (1948):

  ... a man must be allowed to trade under his own name and if some confusion results, that is a lesser evil than that a man should be deprived of ... a natural and inherent right.

The right to use one's own name

Rodgers (Joseph) & Sons v WN Rodgers (1924) imposed qualifications as follows:

(a) the person's full name must be used;

(b) the use must be honest;

(c) nothing must be done to amount to deception;

(d) the name must not be applied to goods.

In *Parker Knoll v Knoll International* (1962) it was held that if goods are marked with the name and there is a likelihood of deception no defence will lie.

There is no defence for using abbreviated names or nicknames (*Biba Group Ltd v Biba Boutique* (1980)).

Figure 5.4

NAMES

✔ **Full name**

✔ **Honest**

✔ **No deception**

✔ **Not used on goods**

Damage

Proof of damage is necessary in an action for passing off. A key task of the courts is to determine the types of damage of which a plaintiff can and cannot complain (*Hodgkinson & Corby Ltd v Wards Mobility* (1994)).

Where a trade rival adopts a name or get-up with fraudulent intent, the court may readily infer damage (*Harrods Ltd v R Harrod Ltd* (1923)), but even if deception can be shown it does not necessarily follow that there is damage (*Stringfellow v McCain Oven Foods (GB)* (1984)).

Actionable damage can be reduced to three types:

(a) diversion of custom;

(b) damage to reputation;

(c) damage by association leading to a dilution of reputation.

Diversion of custom

The most common form of damage is diversion of trade from the plaintiff to the defendant, with the resultant loss of sales. This covers so called classical passing off where a defendant represents his goods as those of another, so a customer who would have bought from the plaintiff is deceived into buying from the defendant instead. To succeed in a claim the parties must usually be competitors to some extent or at least engaged in the same type of industry (*Albion Motor Car Co v Albion Carriage and Motor Body Works Ltd* (1917)).

Loss of sales may be direct or indirect. In *Hoffman La Roche v DDSA* (1969), coloured pills were sold to pharmaceutical retailers and then to the public. Although the initial purchasers were not deceived by the imitation, the fact that the colours were recognised by the public could lead to a loss of sales, even though they did not know the identity of the original manufacturer.

In *Draper v Twist* (1939), it was held that if a defendant puts a quantity of goods on the market which are to be taken as those of the plaintiff, the court will infer some loss of sales without the plaintiff having to prove the necessary transactions.

Where a defendant has deliberately sought to deceive the public, the court will usually assume that he has succeeded (*Lever v Bedingfield* (1898),) although each case will turn on its particular facts.

Damage to reputation
Damage to reputation is a long-standing cause of action but can be hard to prove. In *Harrods Ltd v R Harrod Ltd* (1923), Warrington LJ stated: 'I think that under the word "property" may be included the trade reputation of the plaintiffs, and that, if tangible injury is shown to the trade reputation of the plaintiffs that is enough.' Included within this can be a wide range of deceptive conduct:

(a) inducing a belief that one class of the plaintiff's goods are of another class or quality (*Teacher v Levy* (1905));

(b) passing off seconds as primary manufacture (*Gillette Safety Razor Ltd v Franks* (1924));

(c) selling stale goods as fresh ones (*Wiltshire United Dairy v Thomas Robinson & Sons Ltd* (1957)).

The likelihood of damage to reputation must be a serious one. In *Blazer v Yardley* (1992), an action by the plaintiff failed to obtain an injunction against the defendants who were well known manufacturers of perfume and toiletries. There was no evidence that the public would think any the worse of the plaintiff by the use of the well known name Blazer in such a context.

If there is no danger of the public being confused no action will lie (*Granada Group Ltd v Ford Motor Co Ltd* (1972); *Miss World v James Street Productions* (1981)). In the latter case, the organisers of the Miss World contest failed to restrain the promoters of *The Alternative Miss World* a film featuring transvestites and shown on the same night as the contest.

See, also, *Harrods v Harrodian School* (1996), above, p 104.

Dilution

Dilution of goodwill provides an alternative claim where there is no common field of activity between the parties, or where the use of a distinctive mark or name by the defendant is not likely to prove very detrimental to the plaintiff, but which will, over the years, lead to diminution of reputation, being cumulative in effect.

In *Tattinger v Albev* (1993), the manufacturers of champagne successfully restrained the emergence of English elderflower champagne. The argument, that the appearance on the market of a product with such a name would erode the distinctive reputation of champagne, succeeded. Similar arguments may be used in any case where a well known brand name is applied to a wide range of products, though generally these will be protected by trade marks.

In *Erven Warnink v Townend* (1979), Lord Diplock held:

> In this class or case there are ... two types of damage to be considered, direct loss of sales, illegitimate competition, and a more gradual damage to the plaintiff's business through depreciation of the reputation their goods enjoy.

Other categories of damage have been accepted:

(a) loss of licensing opportunity (*Lego v Lemelstrich* (1983));

(b) risk of litigation (*Walter v Ashton* (1902));

(c) confusion on part of customers and traders (*Chelsea Man v Chelsea Girl* (1987)).

Figure 5.5

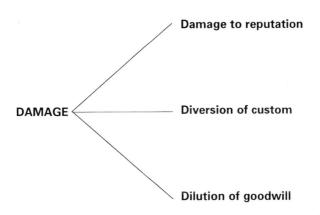

Remedies

As with other intellectual property rights, a successful plaintiff may obtain an injunction, damages or both.

An account of profits is available in the alternative.

Injunctions may be granted on terms.

Damages are treated in a similar way to infringement of registered trade marks. See below, p 133.

6 Malicious falsehood

An action for malicious falsehood may lie in common law for statements which damage the business reputation of another or his goods. The tort is also known as injurious falsehood or trade libel and is triable before a single judge and not before a jury as in libel actions.

Statements may be made orally or in writing (*Ratcliffe v Evans* (1892)) and a plaintiff may also plead libel as well malicious falsehood if the facts may be construed as either (*Joyce v Sengupta* (1993)).

Elements of the tort were set out in *Royal Baking Powder Co v Wright Crossley & Co* (1901):

(a) an untrue statement;

(b) made maliciously;

(c) damage.

These principles were restated in *Kaye v Robertson* (1990).

In *Atkins v Perrin* (1862), it was held that the court has to decide as a matter of fact:

* whether the defendant's belief was a genuine one;

* if genuine, whether it was one a reasonable man might hold.

Where a defendant honestly believes a statement is true, but it is in fact false, there will be no malice and an action will not lie. Neither will an action lie where a defendant makes a statement carelessly, but without any intention of harming the plaintiff (*Balden v Shorter* (1933)).

There must be an untrue statement or real disparagement which a reasonable man would take to be a serious claim (*De Beers Abrasive v International General Electric* (1975)).

If a defendant seeks to justify the statement at the interlocutory stage, no injunction will lie.

In *De Beers*, it was held that a person is entitled to puff his own goods with statements like: 'our goods are better than the plaintiffs.'

A defendant is not entitled to say that the plaintiff's goods are rubbish unless he can establish that the goods are indeed rubbish.

Figure 6.1

ELEMENTS OF MALICIOUS FALSEHOOD

✔ **Malice**

✔ **False statement**

✔ **Damage**

Malice

In relation to malice:

- it must be established that the defendant acted with a 'sinister purpose' (*Seville v Constance* (1954)); or

- malice must be capable of being inferred (*British Railway Traffic and Electric Co Ltd v CRC Co Ltd and LCC* (1922)).

Damage

Proof of damage is necessary to sustain a claim.

In *Dicks v Brooks* (1880), it was held there must be sensible, appreciable damage.

Damage must be a direct and natural consequence of the words used.

In *Wilkinson v Downtown* (1897), the plaintiff recovered costs for medical treatment for shock, following a malicious claim that her husband had been injured.

Until the enactment of the Defamation Act 1952, a plaintiff had to prove special damage. Heads of damage could include diminution in value, loss of particular transactions or licensing opportunities and general trade damage.

Section 3(1) of the Defamation Act 1952 provides that it is not necessary to prove special damage where:

(a) the words are published in written or permanent form and are calculated to cause pecuniary damage to the plaintiff;

(b) the words are calculated to cause pecuniary loss to the plaintiff in respect of trade, office, calling or profession.

7 Character merchandising

The tort of appropriation of personality is recognised as existing in some jurisdictions.

English law provides a collection of rights and remedies whereby personalities, whether real or fictional, may be protected, and this involves a range of intellectual property rights.

Defamation, copyright, passing off, trade marks and malicious falsehood have all been employed on occasion to try to protect a property right deemed as existing in a character, although the English courts have been slow to recognise such rights.

Defamation

At common law, a libel action could be brought to prevent defamatory statements aimed at a person.

Defamation might occur in written descriptions or in drawings or physical caricatures:

- *Monson v Tussauds* (1894): display of an effigy in Madam Tussauds held to be libellous;

- *Tolley v JS Fry* (1931): the reproduction of an image of an amateur golfer held to be libellous.

Copyright

Copyright has failed to protect the names of fictional characters, eg, 'Kojak' in *Taverner Rutledge v Trexapalm* (1975) and 'Wombles' in *Wombles Ltd v Womble Skips* (1977), since names and titles are too short to constitute a work and thereby qualify for copyright protection.

Copyright has been invoked to protect the physical expression of a character, such as a cartoon character depicted in line drawings, eg, *King Features Syndicate v OM Kleeman* (1940) (the 'Popeye' case). However, apart from the interlocutory decision it does not appear to extend to the concept of a character in a literary or artistic work.

Photographs

No right exists to prevent a person photographing another; a person is as free to take photographs as he is to produce a written description (*Sports and General Press Agency v Our Dogs Co Ltd* (1916)).

Certain rights to privacy in photographs are created among the forms of moral rights created under the CDPA 1988.

Trade marks

An attempt to use trade mark protection, in *Re Pussy Galore* (1967), by the estate of Ian Fleming, for the names of 16 characters from the James Bond stories and for the words 'secret agent' failed, as it was not possible to show a *bona fide* intention to use the trade marks applied for.

Trade mark protection will only apply where the mark is being used in a trading context (see *British Sugar plc v James Robertson plc* (1996)).

Passing off

Passing off has been used by both real and fictional personalities to try to protect their 'characters' from exploitation by others:

* *McCulloch v Lewis A May (Produce Distributors) Ltd* (1947): 'Uncle Mac Radio' – personality unable to restrain manufacturers of breakfast cereal who used his name;

- *Sim v HJ Co Ltd* (1959): actor, Alistair Sim, unable to prevent an impersonation of his voice in a commercial.

In *Shaw Brothers (Hong Kong) v Golden Harvest* (1972), the plaintiffs claimed rights in a character 'Fang Kang', the 'one armed swordsman', with regard to passing off in the context of martial arts films.

Other cases involving fictional creations which were not successful before the English courts, include:

- *Taverner Rutledge v Trexapalm* (1975): 'Kojakpops' lollipops could not be restrained by image owners – different field of activity;

- *Lyngstad v Annabas* (1977): pictures of Abba pop group could be used on T-shirts against wishes of owners;

- *Wombles Ltd v Womble Skips* (1977): no passing off in using the word 'Wombles' on rubbish skips.

Cases in other jurisdictions protecting fictional characters have been more successful, see:

- *Pacific Dunlop v Hogan* (1989) and *Hogan v Koala Dundee* (1991): 'Crocodile Dundee';

- *Children's Television Workshop v Woolworths* (1981): 'Sesame Street characters'.

In the UK, the decision in *Mirage Productions v Counter-Feat Clothing* (1991) (concerning 'Ninja Turtles') recognised that licensing of characters was a recognised business practice known to the public and that harm to the goodwill which existed in the plaintiff's turtles could be caused if unlicensed merchandise entered the market.

It therefore follows that both the general elements of passing off must be established together with proof that specific damage may result to the owners of the image from wrongful exploitation of the image.

Figure 7.1

PASSING OFF AS A MEANS OF PROTECTION IN CHARACTER MERCHANDISING

Elements of passing off (see *Erven Warnink v Townend* (1979); *Reckitt v Coleman* (1990))

+

Damage resulting to image or its exploitation

Figure 7.2

CHARACTER MERCHANDISING

No separate tort of appropriation of personality

BUT

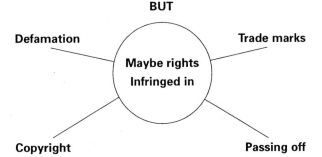

8 Registered trade marks

Registered trade marks guarantee the origin of goods and services.

Originally developed in the 19th century, and now contained in the Trade Marks Act 1994 (TMA), the trade mark registration system protects the rights attaching to a mark in a way which the passing off cannot ensure because of the unpredictability of common law actions. Rights in passing off are expressly preserved by the TMA 1994.

The TMA 1994 implements Council Directive 89/104/EEC, makes provision in connection with the Community Trade Mark (Council Regulation (EC) 40/94) and gives effect to the Madrid Protocol for the Registration of Marks Internationally. The Act operates in the context of the new 'Community' trade mark registration system, which came into effect on 1 April 1996.

The TMA 1994 replaces the Trade Marks Act 1938, but the courts have shown that they will continue to apply case law which arose under the 1938 Act and earlier trade marks legislation.

Restrictions on what may be registered are relaxed by the TMA 1994, allowing almost any indentifier which characterises a business, and which is a feature that the public recognises as distinctive of the business, to be registered, if capable of graphic representation.

Included would be:

(a) letter/numeral combinations (real or invented);

(b) logo marks and business names;

(c) designs;

(d) designs of vehicles;

(e) shapes (subject to s 3(2));

(f) colours;

(g) liveries or shop facades;

(h) sound patterns.

A trade mark takes the form of personal property (s 22). It may be bought, sold or leased or licensed by agreement. Licensing provisions exist under ss 28–31 of the Act allowing a licensee to bring proceedings in specified circumstances. Licences do not have to be in writing.

Advantages of registration

The advantages of registering trade marks include:

(a) greater protection to a mark – no need to prove elements of passing off and reputation;

(b) legal proceedings and dealings are simplified, eg, registration = title;

(c) some disputes may be resolved by the Trade Marks registrar (saving time and expense in litigation – although parties may be represented before the registrar);

(d) a registered mark is protected nationally (and now also within the EU if a Community trade mark), whereas passing off actions may only apply locally;

(e) both consumers and traders benefit from a system of registration which places limits on what constitutes a trade mark.

Proceedings cannot be brought for unregistered marks, though rights of passing off are expressly preserved (s 2(2)). Parties may sue in the alternative.

Figure 8.1

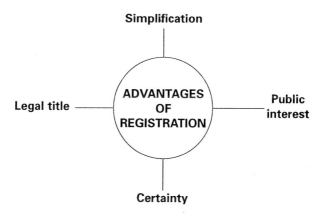

Registration

The system protects any sign which may be capable of being represented graphically (s 1(1)).

The register system is maintained by the Patent Office and is under the control of the registrar.

An application must contain a request for registration, details of the applicant, a statement of the goods and/or services to which the mark is to be applied and a representation of the mark, which means reproduction in graphical form, within a box, 8 cm x 8 cm.

Under the Trade Mark Rules 1994, 42 categories of goods and services are listed for which a trade mark may be registered. Frequently, registration may be sought for more than one category.

The registrar conducts a search of existing marks and examines whether the proposed mark meets the criteria prescribed by law for the application.

Certain absolute grounds exist for refusal of registration, based upon mandatory and optional grounds, laid down in Art 3(1) and (2). No other grounds may be implemented by national law to found a ground for objection to registration.

Absolute grounds include:

(a) failure to satisfy s 1(1) or s 3(1)(a);

(b) the mark is devoid of distinctive character;

(c) the mark consists exclusively of descriptive elements (s 3(1)(c));

(d) the mark has become customary within the established *bona fide* trade.

Limitations are also placed on shapes of containers (s 3(2)).

Further grounds for refusal of registration include (s 3(3)):

(a) marks contrary to public policy;

(b) marks 'of such a nature as to deceive the public';

Section 3(5) provides grounds for refusal where the mark is a specially protected emblem, eg, Royal arms, EU flags and symbols (s 4);

Section 3(6) provides grounds for refusal in cases of bad faith.

Registration will also be refused if there is a conflict with an earlier register entry or an earlier right.

Under s 5, registration will be refused if there is conflict with an earlier identical mark (s 5(1)); or if the conflict is with a similar mark for similar goods, together with the likelihood of confusion and, if the conflict is with a mark that has a reputation, if registration would be unfair or detrimental to that earlier mark (s 5(3)).

Conflict with an unregistered mark (s 5(4)(a)) or other right (s 5(4)(b)) will also prevent registration.

Figure 8.2

TO BE REGISTERABLE A TRADE MARK MUST BE:

- **capable of graphical representation**

- **distinctive**

- **not descriptive**

- **not excluded under the TMA 1994**

The applicant enjoys rights of appeal both to the trade marks registrar and to the courts.

Earlier case law will assist with the meaning of these terms; arguably, the same definitions in s 5 are applicable to the corresponding terms in s 10.

A trade mark can be kept in force indefinitely, providing registration fees are paid and there is an intention to use it (s 32).

Invalidity

A trade mark may be declared invalid under s 47 and removed from the register.

The application may be made by any person and may be made to the registrar or the court (s 47(3)), unless court proceedings are already taking place.

Invalidity proceedings may remove a mark from registration for all or some of its of the relevant registrations (s 47(5)).

Grounds for revocation

Figure 8.3

INVALIDITY UNDER SECTION 47

Invalid if:

- **breach of s 1**

- **breach of s 3**

- **breach of s 5**

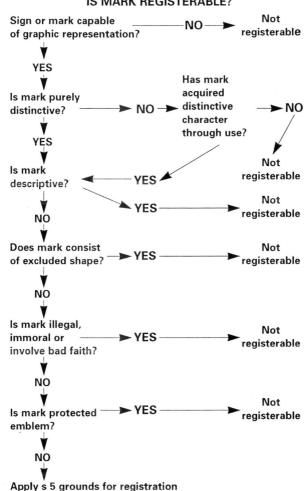

Figure 8.4

IS MARK REGISTERABLE?

Sign or mark capable of graphic representation? —— NO ——▶ Not registerable

↓ YES

Is mark purely distinctive? ——▶ NO ——▶ Has mark acquired distinctive character through use? ——▶ NO

↓ YES

Is mark descriptive? ◀—— YES ◀——

Not registerable

Is mark descriptive? ——▶ YES ——▶ Not registerable

↓ NO

Does mark consist of excluded shape? ——▶ YES ——▶ Not registerable

↓ NO

Is mark illegal, immoral or involve bad faith? ——▶ YES ——▶ Not registerable

↓ NO

Is mark protected emblem? ——▶ YES ——▶ Not registerable

↓ NO

Apply s 5 grounds for registration

INTELLECTUAL PROPERTY LAW

Rights in a trade mark and infringement

Section 9 of the TMA 1994, provides exclusive rights to the proprietor of the trade mark in the UK. Section 9 introduces the infringement provisions of ss 10–13 which specify rights and effects of infringement. The licensing provisions under ss 28–31 of the Act allow a licensee to bring proceedings in specified circumstances. Licences do not have to be in writing.

A mark is protected from unauthorised use, which is defined, by s 103(2), as including use otherwise than by means of a graphic representation, eg, oral representations.

Section 9 rights have effect from the date of registration of the mark (s 40(3)), which is the date of filing of the application for registration). Infringement proceedings cannot begin until registration occurs (*Origins Natural Resources Inc v Origin Clothing Ltd* (1995)).

In proceedings, the Rules of the Supreme Court (Amendment No 3) 1995 provides that, in infringement proceedings, the party against whom the claim is made may, in his defence, put in issue the validity of a mark or revocation of a mark, or raise it as a counterclaim.

The infringement section stems from Art 5 of the Directive.

Primary acts of infringement arise through use (s 10(1)).

Secondary acts of infringement require knowledge (s 10(5)).

Figure 8.5

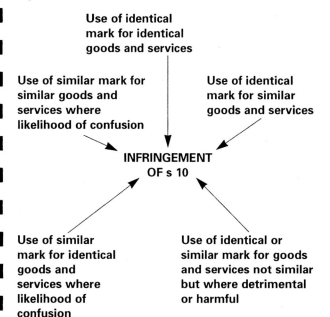

Under s 10(1), no evidence of confusion is needed if an identical mark is used on identical goods.

For proceedings under s 10(2), where the marks and the goods or services are identical or similar, the ambit of infringement is beyond the protection provided by the Trade Marks Act 1938.

The mark or the goods need not be identical, only similar where there is a likelihood of confusion of the public.

Arguably, concepts and tests of similarity relevant to s 10(2) are the same as those for s 5.

Likelihood of confusion of the public is a fundamental requirement and may be shown by evidence, but remains a separate legal test, see similarity discussion, pp 129–32.

Comparison is made between the mark as registered and the alleged infringement used in relation to the particular goods and services actually concerned. Comparison is on a 'sign for sign' basis (*British Sugar plc v James Robertson plc* (1996)) and it will not assist a defendant to claim that there is no likelihood of confusion due to the distinguishing matter surrounding the mark as it is actually used.

The provision has no application where goods and services are not similar and does not overlap with s 10(3). Goods are either similar or not – there is no middle ground.

Section 10(3) provides a wholly new ground of infringement where a sign is used which is identical to or similar to a registered trade mark which has a reputation in the UK for goods or services that are not similar, eg, putting a registered trade mark for a soft drink with a reputation on a can of weedkiller. It is based on Art 5(2) of the Directive.

Under s 10(3), protection is against the dilution of a distinctive character of a mark. This is a new development in UK law, allowing an action for infringement for use of the mark on goods other than those for which the mark is registered. It is a requirement of infringement that the registered trade mark has a reputation, which is something distinct from goodwill and does not necessarily require any use in the UK.

Protection may only be limited to use in a trade mark sense not to the use of marks (particularly word marks) in any other context (see *British Sugar plc v James Robertson* (1996); *Football Association v Trebor Ltd* (1997)).

Comparative advertising is also caught to prevent one trader riding on the back of another's mark. However, note the words in s 10(6) regarding 'honest practices in industrial and commercial matters'. This provision allows, for instance, consumers to obtain information about different brands which might include the use of a trade mark. As to honest uses in business, see *Baume & Co v Moore* (1958) and *Provident Financial v Halifax Building Society* (1994).

Section 10(6) provides two things for an infringement in law:

(a) use of the mark otherwise than in accordance with honest practices in industrial or commercial matters; and

(b) must without due cause take unfair advantage of, or be detrimental to, the distinctive character or repute of the trade mark.

It follows that comparative advertising may take place if fair.

Limitations are imposed by s 11 of the 1994 Act on the scope of infringement of registered trade mark and details important circumstances where a mark is not infringed, eg, the use by a person of his own name or address (s 11(2)(a)).

A registered mark is not infringed by use in the course of trade in a particular locality of an earlier right which applies only in that locality. An earlier right means an unregistered trade mark or other sign which has been used continuously in relation to goods or services by a person or a predecessor in title, from a date preceding registration, so long as the earlier right had such goodwill as could be protected in a passing off action (s 11(3)).

Under s 16, an application for delivering up is not an infringement proceeding.

Legitimate uses by a non-mark holder

Certain uses of a mark are permitted by a non-owner:

(a) a person's own name and address;

(b) indications of kind, quality, quantity, intended purpose, value, geographical origin, time of production or rendering, or other characteristics of goods or services;

(c) the mark itself, where this is necessary to indicate the intended purpose of a product or service, eg, for spare parts.

However, rights of action may still exist in passing off, which is expressly preserved.

Community trade marks

European Council Regulation 40/94 established the Community Trade Mark registration system. The Community Trade Mark system provides protection for marks throughout the EU.

Opposition

Opposition to a trade mark registration may be commenced either during the application stage or after the mark has been granted.

Any person may apply to oppose the trade mark registration.

Comparing trade marks

Both the courts and the Trade Marks Registry may be called upon to determine whether marks are so confusing with another's registered trade mark with regard to both s 5 and s 10.

Under s 5, the registrar may refuse to register a trade mark which is identical or similar to an existing mark and there is a risk of confusion to the public.

Under s 10, infringement proceedings may be brought by the owner of a trade mark against another who uses an identical or similar mark without licence or consent.

Similarity may also be an issue in cases involving:

(a) applications for revocation or invalidity;

(b) proceedings for the restraint of use of the Royal Arms;

(c) passing off;

(d) prosecutions for unauthorised use of registered trade mark

Each case will turn on its facts.

The relevant facts for comparison are as follows:

(a) the two signs must be taken and judged by their look and sound;

(b) the goods to which the marks are applied and the nature and kind of customer must be considered;

(c) the circumstances of the trade concerned (*Kidax (Shirts) Ltd Application* (1959)) must be looked at.

Consideration is on a 'sign for sign' basis (*James Robertson plc v British Sugar Ltd* (1996)) *per* Jacob J.

With words or name marks the classic test is *Pianotist* (1906), *per* Parker J:

> You must take the two words. You must consider the nature and kind of customer who would be likely to buy these goods. In fact, you must consider all the surrounding circumstances, and you must further consider what is likely to happen if each of those trade marks is used in a normal way as a trade mark for the goods of the respective owners of the mark.

If, following such consideration, the court takes the view that there is a likelihood of confusion, registration may be denied or a finding of infringement will follow.

In *Smith-Hayden & Co Ltd's Application* (1946) *(aka Re Ovax (1946))*:

> ... having regard to the user of the mark applied for: is the tribunal satisfied that the mark, if used in a normal or fair manner in connection with any goods covered by the registration proposed, will not reasonably be likely to cause deception and confusion amongst a substantial number of persons.

Figure 8.6

ASSESSING SIMILARITY OF MARKS PRESUMED

- Normal and fair use of mark

- No deception

- Substantial number of persons

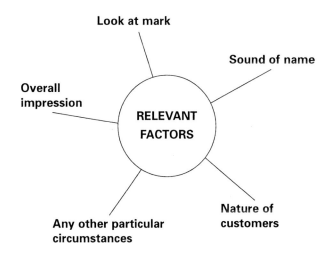

Figure 8.7

SIMILARITY OF GOODS
(Re Jellinek (1946))

- **Nature and composition of goods**

- **Uses to which goods are put**

- **Trade channels through which goods are sold**

Imperfect recollection is a factor to be considered.

It is recognised that marks will rarely be seen side by side (*Reckitt & Coleman Products v Boardman & Co* (1990)).

Deciding whether a mark is similar is related to but not determinative of the question of whether it is likely to confuse (see *The European v The Economist* (1996)).

Customers are deemed to be 'ordinary purchasers purchasing with caution' (*Seixo v Provezende* (1866)).

When considering the impression that the two marks may have, the court ignores extraordinarily stupid or unobservant people ('moron in a hurry' from *Morning Star Co-operative Society Ltd v Express Newspapers* (1979)).

Figure 8.8

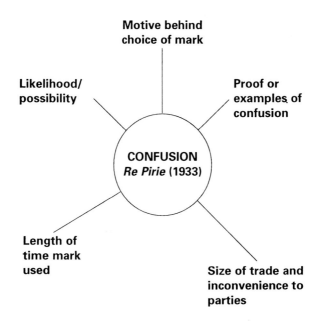

CONFUSION
Re Pirie (1933)

Motive behind choice of mark

Likelihood/ possibility

Proof or examples of confusion

Length of time mark used

Size of trade and inconvenience to parties

Damages

Damages for trade mark infringement are similar to passing off and assessed on similar principles.

Nominal damages lie for an infringing use of a mark (*Blofield v Payne* (1833)).

The plaintiff may claim for the profit on every infringing item without proving that a sale occurred to a deceived consumer (*Lever v Goodwin* (1887)).

In *Alexander v Henry* (1895), damages were awarded for fraudulent use of the plaintiff's mark and loss of sales.

9 Design rights

Designs with 'eye appeal' are registerable under the Registered Designs Act 1949.

Registration is with the Patent Office following prescribed rules on application of the design right owner (s 3).

Section 1 of the Registered Designs Act 1949 as amended, defines registerable designs as being:

> ... features of shape, configuration or ornament applied to an article by any industrial process, being features which in the finished article appeal to and are judged by the eye.

Such appeal 'is that created by the distinctiveness or shape, pattern or ornament calculated to influence the customer's choice' (*Interlego v Tyco Industries Inc* (1988)).

If there is no question of eye appeal, the design will not be registerable under s 1(3).

The design must be one which is applied to an article and must be novel in the sense of being new.

Section 44(1) provides that article means any article of manufacture and includes any part of an article if that part is made and sold separately.

In *Ford Motor Co Ltd's Design Applications* (1995), the House of Lords held that an article should be an independent item intended to be made and sold individually, rather than part of a larger article.

The design right is owned by the person who created it (s 2(1)).

The owner of the design right enjoys exclusive rights in relation to articles encompassing the design.

Infringement is determined by viewing the article through the eyes of the interested consumer

The right subsists for an initial period of five years, renewable at five yearly intervals to a maximum of 25 years.

Unregistered design rights under the CDPA 1988

An unregistered design right is created under s 213(2) of the CDPA 1988.

Under s 213, 'design' means: 'the design of any aspect of the shape or configuration (whether external or internal) of the whole or part of the article.'

The owner of the unregistered design right is entitled to exclusive rights of reproduction. The owner must establish either copying of the design or a substantial part of it (s 226(1)).

Secondary infringement may arise under s 228(1).

To qualify for protection a design must:

(a) be recorded in a document after 1 August 1989;

(b) be original;

(c) not be subject to exclusion;

(d) qualify for protection under s 213(5).

Where an article is made to a design in which the design right subsists or has subsisted, the court will act on the presumption that the article was made at a time when the right subsisted, unless the contrary can be proved.

Originality requires that the design must not be commonplace in the area of design in question (s 213(4)) and must originate with the designer and not have been copied.

(See *C & H Engineering v Klucznic* (1992)).

The design right subsists in the design for 15 years from when it was recorded in a document, unless articles have been made available for sale, in which case, the period is limited to 10 years.

A number of exceptions exist, under s 213, to the entitlement to protection.

The design right will not arise in the following excluded categories under s 213:

(a) principles of construction;

(b) where the article has features that enable it to be connected, placed in or around another article to perform a function ('must fit');

(c) designs that depend on the appearance of another article ('must match');

(d) surface decoration.

Exceptions (b) and (c) are particularly relevant to the manufacturers of spare parts.

Figure 9.1

EXCLUDED CATEGORIES UNDER s 213

- **Method or principle of construction**

- **Shapes or configurations which are functional ('must fit')**

- **Dependent on appearance of another item ('must match')**

- **Surface decoration**